D1325517

NYMPH FISHING
IN PRACTICE

By

OLIVER KITE

BARRIE & JENKINS

COMMUNICA-EUROPA

© Oliver Kite 1963

First published by Herbert Jenkins Limited
Reprinted 1969
Reprinted 1977 by Barrie & Jenkins Limited
24 Highbury Crescent London N5 1RX

ISBN 0 257 66124 7

Printed and bound in Great Britain by
REDWOOD BURN LIMITED
Trowbridge & Esher

Contents

List of Illustrations

7

Illustrations in the Text

Maps

Photographs 1, 2, and 16 are reproduced by permission of E. Horsfall Turner, and photographs 4, 6, 8 and 15 are by permission of "The Field": to both the author offers grateful thanks.

Acknowledgements

I WISH to acknowledge my debt to all those who have helped me, directly and indirectly, with the preparation of this book. I should like to thank especially: Mr. Ian Wood, Editor of *Trout and Salmon*, for his invaluable advice when the book was first conceived, and for permission to make use of material from my contributions published in his magazine; Mr. L. G. Pine, Managing Editor of *The Shooting Times*, for permission to use extracts from "Fisherman's Diary" published in that weekly; Mr. Eric Horsfall Turner, Editor of *Anglers' Annual*, for help with photographs and permission to make use of statistics which appeared in that annual; Mr. Kenneth Mansfield, Editor of *Angling*, Captain Wilson Stephens, Editor of *The Field*, and Miss Patricia Marston, Editor of *The Fishing Gazette*, for permission to make use of material which I first contributed to their magazines in another form; and Major R. E. C. Escombe, Editor of *The Salmon and Trout Magazine*, for permission to reproduce a figure contributed to his magazine by Dr. T. T. Macan and for kindly allowing me to quote dates from the appendices of my paper, *The Emergence of Ephemeropteran Subimagines in 1961*.

I am grateful to Dr. T. T. Macan of The Freshwater Biological Association and to Messrs. Longmans, Green & Co. Limited for permission to make use of figures (Figs. 1 to 8 in this book) from Dr. Macan's book, *A Guide to Freshwater Invertebrates*. I should also like to thank Dr. Macan, Dr. Michael Wade of Risca, Mon., and Mr. C. M. B. Harrisson of Queen's College, Cambridge, for their help in revising the appendix dealing with the classification of natural nymphs.

I should like to thank all those who kindly allowed me access to study insect life in their waters, and especially Mr.

Alex Behrendt of Romsey, Commander J. S. Douglas, R.N., of Woodford Bridge, North Devon, Mr. Stanley Hesketh of Blackburn, Major and the Hon. Mrs. Robert Heywood-Lonsdale of Bapton, and Lieutenant-Colonel Alan Lane, Hon. Secretary of the Officers' Fishing Association.

I should also like to acknowledge the help and advice of various kinds which I have been given by Wing Commander Anthony Coke of Heytesbury, Mr. William B. Currie of Edinburgh, Mr. Alan Dalton of Over Wallop, Dr. James Drummond of Salisbury, Mr. Ernest Mott of Longstock, Captain George Old of Blackburn, Mr. David Sumner of Lytham St. Annes, Commander C. F. Walker, R.N., of Heathfield, Mr. William Walmsley of Blackburn, and Mr. T. K. Wilson of Skipton.

This book would be incomplete without an acknowledgement of the immeasurable debt which I, and many other present-day fly-fishers, owe to the late Mr. G. E. M. Skues, to whom nymph fishing, as such, owed its inception. The successful establishment of nymph fishing as an accepted method of fly-fishing, to be employed in conjunction with the art of the dry-fly, is wholly attributable to Skues's powers of observation and deduction, his creative ability, his masterly, persuasive and fair-minded presentation of his theories, discoveries and fishing philosophy, and above all his moral courage in holding fast in the face of the most formidable opposition to what he believed to be both sporting and logical.

Finally I should like to pay a special tribute to my wife, Norah, who collaborated with me throughout the preparation of this book, undertook most of the hard work, typed, criticised and revised the drafts and manuscript, and dealt with the immense correspondence entailed. Without her help and inspiration over the years this book could not have been written.

Introduction

I HAVE been interested in fishing as long as I can remember. I think my first fish was a Severn gudgeon but I cut my angler's teeth on roach in a Monmouthshire pond. There, too, I caught my first trout, on bread paste. My second took a worm when I was eel fishing in the same county. Later, when my family moved to Lancashire, I learned the more delicate art of clear-water upstream worming for beck trout.

The main lesson I absorbed from the much-fished waters of that populous county was that to catch good fish of any species, whether they be trout or roach, handsome perch or shy tench, concealing one's presence and intentions from them is an essential prerequisite for consistent success.

When the war came and I went into the Army, opportunities for fishing were decidedly limited for a few years but they did arise from time to time, even among the chaungs of Arakan and North Burma. Then came the invasion of Malaya, the occupation of Siam and a spell in Singapore before I went back to India to join my regiment in Fort William, Calcutta, shortly after Independence Day. Conveniently, the well-stocked Havildar's Tank was situated right outside the old walls.

Wherever my service took me, I enjoyed such fishing as was available, often improvising tackle to do so, in rivers, lakes, tanks, swamps, streams and, of course, the sea. The game fishes of the warm seas off Sierra Leone and Gambia were my last quarry before I returned to England in 1953 for the Coronation procession. In the summer of that year

I first came to the Upper Avon in Wiltshire, temporarily on the staff of the 42nd (Lancashire) Infantry Division (T.A.) which was carrying out large-scale manœuvres on Salisbury Plain. Except for the operational crossing problems to which it gave rise, the river made little impression on me at the time.

Yet this had been the country of my forbears. My grandfather, William Kite (1859–1950), was born at Market Lavington on the edge of the Plain and lived there as a child until my great-grandfather moved to Monmouthshire. He, George Kite, was christened on New Year's Eve, 1820, in Heytesbury church beside the Wylye. My great-greatgrandfather, William, and his forefathers before him, lived in the Wylye valley and knew, and doubtless loved, the rivers of the Plain as I do now. My son did not survive and now our male saga is almost done. Meanwhile the wheel has turned full circle, fortuitously bringing me to live beside the Avon which divides the Plain.

At the beginning of 1955, I was posted from the Staff College at Camberley to the 2nd Infantry Brigade at Bulford, with the modest but resounding appointment of Deputy Assistant Adjutant- and Quartermaster-general. That year I got to know the Upper Avon very well, by night and day, and all the broad rolling downs of the Plain over which we constantly exercised our brigade headquarters and administrative echelons. The following year, having the job under control and hoping to find some spare time in which to fish, I took a half-rod on the Officers' Fishing Association water which includes most of the six miles of the Avon from Bulford up to Coombe Mill. This entitled me to one day's fishing per week, dry-fly or upstream nymph only.

I took to chalk-stream fly-fishing from the start, though I didn't find it easy at first. I read a great deal, steeping myself in the lore and traditions of this somewhat esoteric branch of angling. The Wylye I soon mastered but the Upper Avon yielded her trout to me grudgingly, one at a time, and only once that first season did I take home a brace. I caught all my fish on the dry-fly. When fish weren't rising I was content to be by the quiet river, at peace.

My first Avon season ended prematurely and abruptly early in August that year when I was flown out to the nuclear weapon-testing range at Maralinga in the desert outback of South Australia to witness and experience a nuclear test explosion. Owing to weather conditions, the test did not take place until the end of September, but the time I spent in that superficially desolate place was one of the most interesting I have ever known, as a layman with a fondness for natural history. But of course there was no water there, and no fish.

Owing to the lack of water and anticipated laundry difficulties, we had been told to take with us pretty well all we possessed in the way of uniforms with vast stocks of plain clothes. One evening early in September when I was away from my tent, in working overalls, it caught fire and all I had in Australia went up in flames. So it was that I arrived in Sydney on October 1st, en route for home via Auckland and some fishing in the North Island of New Zealand, in a borrowed Australian battledress, black boots and a bush-whacker's hat.

I never got to Auckland, Taupo and the rest. A few hours after reaching Sydney I had a heart attack and was carted off to hospital at Concord overlooking the Parramatta River where the kindest people I've ever met looked after me devotedly. My luck seemed to be running out. I thought a lot about the Avon in the months which followed and wondered if I should ever see and hear those waters of comfort again.

But when the 1957 season opened, I was safely back in Bulford, ready and anxious to try conclusions with the Avon trout again. Now, however, I stood a better chance. My active military career was over. The sword was sheathed and henceforth I was to earn my bread with the pen, writing Infantry Training manuals. But for some months during my sick leave, my time was to be my own. My duty, I had been told, was to get out into the air and get well. I intended to comply with these orders and at the same time apply myself to acquiring some of the more sophisticated rudiments of the chalk-stream fly-fisher's art.

When things were quiet when I was fishing at Choulston one day in the 1957 season, I thought I might do better if I went higher up and tried my hand with a nymph. I had shop nymphs which I didn't consider worth using. Besides these I had also a couple of Sawyer's small pheasant-tail nymphs and off I went to see what I could do. Above Choulston is the famous Court Reach at Netheravon, just at the back of the cottage where I now live. There, below Haxton Bridge, I found a good trout swinging to and fro in a streamy current where it emerged from between two clumps of starwort.

This trout refused various dry-flies. I put on one of the small nymphs I had been given, casting it accurately a few feet ahead of the trout. As it passed the fish's head without being taken, I raised the tip of my rod to withdraw it. As I did so I saw the trout turn, so I stayed my hand momentarily then, as the trout turned back, I struck. And that was how I caught my first trout on the artificial nymph. That was also the inspiration of my nymph-fishing technique, developed, modified, tested and regularly practised during the succeeding years.

I only use this one pattern of nymph, the one I began with, anywhere. I have not yet found any other necessary. This book sets out my concept of the Netheravon style of nymph fishing, the manner in which I practise the art, and relates some occasions when it has proved outstandingly successful on various waters and, as is right, includes a note of some circumstances in which it proved less effective.

I have tried in this book to answer the questions most often put to me by fly-fishers who attend my classes and lectures or in discussions on the river bank and elsewhere. I can only give worthwhile answers in the context of my own personal experience. I do not wish to present this book as a universal guide to nymph fishing: I doubt if any man could write such a tome, or if he would be believed if he tried. I am not trying to teach my brother anglers their trade. But I hope my own experiences with this fascinating branch of fly-fishing will prove to be both interesting and encouraging to those who find that nymph fishing presents problems in actual practice.

Natural Nymphs

WHAT IS A NYMPH?

Wнат is a nymph, a natural nymph, in the context of fly-fishing terminology? What type of insects emerge from nymphs? During which phase of their life cycle do nymphs occur and at what stage of this phase may they properly be so termed? What do nymphs look like, where are they to be found, and how do they behave?

You do not need to know the answers to all these questions to be able to catch fish on an artificial nymph, any more than you need to know much about entomology to catch fish on the dry-fly. Given suitable artificial representations and a knowledge of the practical application of modern nymph-fishing technique, there is no reason why anyone who possesses normal dry-fly fishing tackle and equipment should not catch trout on nymphs when the situation is propitious. If you do know the answers, however, the act of nymph fishing straightaway becomes more intelligible. Quite apart from the added interest, you are better equipped to know when to employ your artificials, how to handle them to effective advantage, where and in what manner to present them, and the most likely reaction to be expected from the fish you are trying to catch.

This immediately opens up to you a number of purposeful courses of action, each giving you the opportunity of practising the fine art of deception by persuading fish that your artificial is *behaving* as well as looking like a natural nymph in the water. To take fish in this manner is profoundly satisfying, whether they be trout, grayling or coarse fish of various species.

Nymph fishing is not necessarily the most effective way of catching fish. On the chalk-stream especially, the dry-fly may be considered more effective at certain times of the year. At other times, more especially in the daytime during the summer months, trout tend to feed more on nymphs than on hatched fly; and when this is the case, nymph fishing enables the angler to enjoy skilful and rewarding sport, while those using only the dry-fly either remain inactive or are relatively unprofitably engaged.

What, then, is the natural nymph which gives rise to this intriguing branch of fly-fishing? The term "nymph" is loosely applied by people interested in natural history to the underwater larval forms of a variety of different families of insects, among them such familiar creatures as dragon-flies, damsel-flies and stone-flies. To the nymph fisherman, how-ever, the term has an altogether more precise meaning. Before defining and explaining this, it might be as well to establish just where and how nymphs fit in in the insect world.

Insects are invertebrate animals possessing six legs. They are of two main kinds—winged and wingless. There are altogether eleven different orders of winged insects, several of which are of interest to fly-fishers, but only one of which concerns the nymph fisherman. This is the order of aquatic upwinged flies or *Ephemeroptera*. It is to these insects, at a certain specific underwater stage in their metamorphosis, that fishermen give the name of nymphs. A brief description of the life cycle of upwinged flies will help to explain what this stage is and just when it occurs.

LIFE CYCLE OF UPWINGED FLIES

The egg

An upwinged fly begins life as an egg which may be laid over, on or in the water, according to species. The time spent in the egg stage varies greatly from species to species, place to place, and season to season. One of the commonest upwinged flies, the Large Olive (*Baëtis rhodani*), lays eggs in September and October, some of which certainly do not hatch until the following year. Temperature seems to affect the time taken by eggs to hatch, for the spring generation of Large Olives lay eggs which hatch considerably quicker than those laid in the autumn.

Some species spend a considerable period in the egg stage, probably to safeguard them during periods of the year unfavourable to later stages. It is still not certain, however, whether the duration of the egg stage is governed by outside influences or embodied factors.

The eggs of some upwinged species may hatch very quickly indeed, more especially if the adult females delay their egg-laying after mating and fertilization has taken place. The Apricot Spinner, which is the beautiful adult female of the Slow-water Olive (*Cloëon dipterum*), may delay laying her eggs after fertilization until they have actually begun to hatch out in her oviducts. When this happens, this species may be regarded as virtually viviparous.

The larvula

The young of an upwinged fly, whether they hatch normally from an egg in the water or are extruded from the parental oviducts as described above, are creatures of minute size termed larvulae. The larvulae of the majority of British upwinged species are very tiny indeed and at this early stage in their life cycle there is little hope of identifying the individual species with certainty, even under microscopic examination. A number of the physical characteristics which will later appear as the insect develops in the water are either wholly lacking or only partially formed in the larvulal phase.

The larvula itself grows by a process of moulting, sloughing its outer skin completely as it does so. Each such moult constitutes a further stage in the insect's development. Successive stages are termed instars and a larvula is said to be in its first instar, second instar, and so on.

These early instars are of comparatively short duration.

Some may last only a few days. After about four such instars, the larvula attains a degree of development sufficient
to justify it thereafter being termed a larva.

The larva

The larva continues to grow by shedding its outer skin as
described. This skin consists largely of sclerotin, a substance
which sets hard when it comes into contact with water.
Once its skin has hardened, therefore, the larva is confined
within it, as though in a strait-jacket, and thereafter can
only expand or change its external physical appearance by
undergoing a further moult.

In some species, growth is fairly continuous. In others it
may be regulated by external factors. The larva of the
Olive Upright (*Rhithrogena semicolorata*) has been observed to
grow throughout the winter months, apparently little
affected by temperature, whereas the larva of the Dusky
Yellowstreak (*Heptagenia lateralis*) ceased growth at the
coldest part of the winter.

Periodic moulting is necessitated not only by growth
resulting from feeding but by impending structural changes.
Internal growth is accompanied by internal development of
physical appendages beneath each successive new skin. Only
by the release made possible by a moult can these new and
somewhat compressed appendages expand.

Quite one of the most obvious of these structural changes
is occasioned by the growth of the insect's wing cases. The
appearance of these on the dorsal thorax, which thereafter
begins to take on its characteristic "hump", is especially
significant to the fly-fisher because they denote the arrival
of the larva at the stage when it may properly be termed a
nymph.

The nymph

Nymphs vary a good deal in size, according to species.
In this country, nymphs of the largest species, the Mayflies
(*Ephemera* spp.), are roughly as large as wasp grubs. At the
other end of the scale, nymphs of the tiny Broadwing species

(*Caenis* spp.) are appreciably smaller than the maggots of house-flies.

Nymphs also vary considerably in general appearance. Although they share a common basic physical structure, the various species differ in detailed make-up owing to adaptations related to their habitat and general behaviour. Typical of these varieties are the streamlined active swimming forms which occur in both still and flowing water, burrowing forms which inhabit the beds of rivers and some lakes, and squat, clinging forms found in fast, rocky rivers and on the stony shores of big lakes. These adaptations and their relation to the habitat of nymphs will be discussed in greater detail later in this chapter. The nymphs of certain species feature more prominently in the diet of fish than others, as will later become quite clear. It is with these nymphs that the nymph fisherman is most concerned in his preparation of suitable artificials and the technique for employing them to realistic effect.

Also of great significance to the nymph fisherman is the fact that individual nymphs of certain species, especially those which are of the greatest importance in nymph fishing, differ considerably from other nymphs of the same species. A typical example is afforded by the nymphs of the Slow-water Olive (*C. dipterum*) which are found in still as well as slow-flowing water and were noted in static-water tanks in cities during the war. These vary considerably, one from another, especially in coloration and superficial appearance. The different stages of development of the wing cases contribute to this and the nymphs range in tone from very pale to very dark, with combinations and permutations in between these extremes.

Now it would be quite impracticable for the fly-dresser to undertake direct imitation of all these varieties, not only of one species but of many, even if this were necessary to enable the nymph fisherman to catch fish. It isn't; a matter of some convenience to the practical angler. The different types of nymphs will be considered in more detail later in this chapter.

The food of the nymphs of upwinged flies principally consists of plant remains and suchlike detritus, diatoms, filamentous algae and similar minute vegetable organisms. The larvae graze on these substances where they have been trapped after being filtered from the current by weed growing in rivers, or by mosses on stones, or by the rough surfaces of stones and boulders themselves, or on the bottom of still or sluggish waters on which they have come to rest.

Being mainly herbivorous creatures, the jaws of nymphs are not well adapted for defensive purposes and the creatures must therefore rely on other means of protecting themselves. Various defensive measures are employed: burrowing, as in the case of the nymphs of Mayflies; camouflage, either by developing protective coloration as in the nymphs of the Claret dun (*Leptophlebia vespertina*) or by collecting detritus and fine silt in minute hairs of the body, as in the tiny nymphs of the Broadwings (*Caenis* spp.); hiding by penetrating deep into weed trash or, in the absence of this, by concealment among mosses on stones, like the nymphs of the Blue-winged Olive (*Ephemerella ignita*); and darting through the water at high speed or, alternatively, sudden movement followed by instant stillness, two methods employed by nymphs of the *Baëtidae* family, which includes the Olives, Iron Blues, Spurwings, Slow-water Olives and other species of special importance to the nymph fisherman.

Nymphs breathe by extracting oxygen from water taken into the body through openings and subsequently diffused. In running water, the natural current normally ensures the presence of adequate dissolved oxygen in the water, but in still conditions, the nymphs must create such a current for themselves by literally fanning the water around them with the so-called tracheal gills, a prominent feature along the flanks of some species. Many species occurring in fast-flowing water are unable to perform this fanning act, for they lack adequate appendages and cannot therefore live in still water.

All British upwinged species have three tail filaments in the nymph stage. Contrary to widespread belief, this is not the case with all Ephemeropterans. A well-known American species, the Floridan Slow-water Olive (*Pseudocloëon alachua* Berner), for example, has only two.

When a nymph reaches maturity, it eventually undergoes an important moult which results in the emergence of the winged insect. This winged form is, however, not the final stage of the upwinged fly. It is known to entomologists as a subimago and to fishermen as a dun.

The subimago or dun

A dun closely resembles the nymph from which it emerges in general structural appearance except, of course, that it has wings and is capable of flight. Duns have large fore-wings and most have small hindwings. In some species (*Cloëon* and *Procloëon*) the hindwings are atrophied and absent, while the two Spurwings (*Centroptilum* spp.) have only narrow rudimentary hindwings, scarcely visible to the naked human eye. The wings of duns are coated with fine hairs.

Some British species have three tails in their winged stages, the same as the nymphs, but rather more have only two tails. In these latter species, the median filament has virtually disappeared. Both sexes of each British species are constant in this respect and, except in cases of deformity through misadventure, both males and females of individual species have either two or three tails, a useful aid to identifica-tion. This convenient feature is not universal. Certain Australian upwinged flies (of the genus *Atalophlebia*), for example, have two tails in the male and three in the female, and in these circumstances it is easy to see that recognition may present additional problems.

Most duns are not particularly colourful insects for they have yet to undergo a final moult. Their rather drab appearance has given rise to the name dun, by which they are generally known to fishermen. The dun stage is purely transitional. The mouth parts are already atrophied and the insect is unable to eat or drink. In most cases it is not yet capable of mating.[1]

[1] The possibility exists that female duns of the Pale Evening dun (*Procloëon pseudorufulum*) mate with impatient adult male imagines of that species. I have

The final moult or ecdysis to attain the adult or imago stage may take place anything from a few minutes to several days after the dun emerges. Some of the Broadwings (*Caenis* spp.) moult almost immediately after emerging. I have known several other species wait a week before moulting. . At other times, especially in dry warm weather, these species may moult within 24 hours.

The final moult usually takes place in the herbage or bushes in the vicinity of the water from which the dun emerged. It is here that the dun rests between the time it leaves the water and the moment when it transposes into an adult fly which fishermen call a spinner. If you catch duns at the waterside, either by netting them from the surface when they first emerge or collecting them from the herbage in which they are resting, you can take them home in a convenient box or tube and, if you keep a close eye on them, study the whole process of this final moult at first hand. Put one or two pipe cleaners into the box with them so that they have something to stick their claws into. The insect which emerges from the dun in this final ecdysis is a beautiful iridescent creature, altogether more diaphanous and colourful than the subimago. All British upwinged species undergo this final moult.

The imago or spinner

The adult spinner has as its function the perpetuation of the species. Males and females differ from one another in a number of obvious respects. The male has long forelegs and a pair of claspers at the tip of the abdomen to enable it to seize and hold the female during the mating act which takes place in the air. Females are sometimes larger than males and their eyes are usually less prominent. The males assemble at the waterside, "dancing" in characteristic swarms whilst awaiting the arrival of the females to be mated. After fertilization, females proceed to the water to lay their eggs.

---

seen this happen on a number of occasions. Whether such unions are fertile has yet to be determined.

The males return to their swarms and comparatively few die over the water.

Spent fly

After oviposition is completed, the spent females are borne away, exhausted, dying and lifeless, by the current. In these circumstances, fish find them easy prey as they float down in the surface film with outstretched wings. Fishermen call these females spent fly. There are times when the nymph fisherman can take advantage of their presence in the water.

BASIC STRUCTURE OF NATURAL NYMPHS

Anyone who has never seen a natural nymph can picture its general appearance by calling to mind a silverfish, the familiar little creature which attacks old books. However, nymphs vary a good deal in size and shape, according to species, some being short and squat and others much bigger, looking vaguely like earwigs. Some have short tails; others have long tails, in relation to the length of their bodies.

The basic structural make-up of a natural nymph, whatever its species, is a small head, a thorax consisting of three segments and an abdomen of ten and, in all British species, three tails.

The head capsule carries a pair of minute antennae, a pair of distinctive eyes, and complex mouthparts. These afford useful taxonomic indications to the identity of certain species.

The thorax comprises three segments each bearing a pair of legs, giving the nymph the six legs characteristic of an insect. The wing cases on the dorsal thorax give to that part of the body a distinctly humped appearance. The size of these wing cases and the degree of hump to which they give rise determines whether the nymph is young, half-grown or full-grown, but the practical nymph fisherman need hardly concern himself with such niceties, unless he is collecting specimens for some reason and wishes to obtain these in a certain stage of development.

The abdomen consists of ten segments. There are fan-like organs on each side of all but the terminal segments which are usually called tracheal gills. The construction, appearance and function of these gills varies considerably between different species.

At the tip of the abdomen are the nymph's three tails. These vary in length in relation to the nymph's body, according to species, and their detailed construction is considerably influenced by the nymph's habitat and general behaviour.

Full-grown nymphs of British species may be recognized by relative size and development of the wing cases, and by signs of emptiness in the median tail filament in those species which have only two tails in the winged stages.

TYPES OF NATURAL NYMPHS

All British species of nymphs may be considered to belong to one of six main types:

> Bottom burrowers;
> Silt crawlers;
> Moss creepers;
> Stone clingers;
> Laboured swimmers; and
> Agile darters.

The allocation of the various British species to each type is given in detail in the appendix at the end of this book.

Bottom burrowers

Among British species, only the nymphs of the three Mayflies (*Ephemera* spp.) are bottom burrowers. They are large nymphs, reaching an overall length of 24–25 mm (1 inch). Mayfly nymphs are suitably adapted for tunnelling in sand, fine gravel and firm silt and for life in such a habitat. They have small, pointed heads, powerful mandibles, strong forelegs for burrowing, mole-fashion, and rather long,

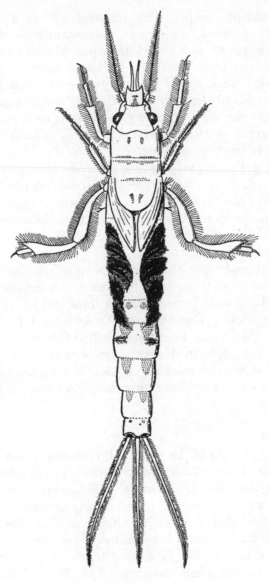

Fig. 1

A bottom burrower: the nymph of the Mayfly
(*Ephemera danica*)

slender, tube-like bodies. The tracheal gills of a Mayfly
nymph are designed to maintain a constant flow of water
around the nymph in its deep burrow. Mayflies occur in
both rivers and lakes, especially limestone lakes.

For a long time, it was generally supposed that the life
cycle of the Mayfly from the time the egg was laid until the
adult was on the wing was two years. Some even say three.
The researches of Dr. Gertrud Pleskot in Austria suggest
that in that country, at least, *E. danica*, the Mayfly most
often seen in Britain, may have a life cycle lasting only one
year. Indeed, it is conceivable that some British Mayfly
nymphs may emerge as duns after only a year. I saw a male
Mayfly emerge on the Wylye at Bapton on November 30th
1961. Had that fly come from an egg laid in May 1961,
May 1960 or May 1959?

Mayfly nymphs quit their burrows to rise to the surface
to emerge as duns, though it is not customary among fishermen to refer to these large insects as duns. They are called
simply Mayflies, or Greendrakes. Trout often take Mayfly
nymphs as they reach the surface. When they feed greedily
on these big nymphs in this way, catching them on a large
artificial nymph can scarcely be dignified by the name of
sport. Those who want fish rather than sport can catch them
in this way.

Silt crawlers

The tiny nymphs of the various Broadwings (*Caenis* spp.)
are slow crawlers inhabiting the surface of silt and mud.
The River Broadwing (*C. macrura*) is found only in running
water, sometimes occurring in the slower reaches of chalk-
streams and other rivers. A minute species, the Brook
Broadwing (*C. rivulorum*), is found in smaller streams, mostly
of a stony character, like becks and burns. I have not seen
it myself in the chalk country. The Black Broadwing
(*C. moesta*) occurs in both still and slow-flowing water, as does
the Yellow Broadwing (*C. horaria*). A recently discovered
species, the Dusky Broadwing (*C. robusta*), has so far only been
identified in this country from a few still waters in South and

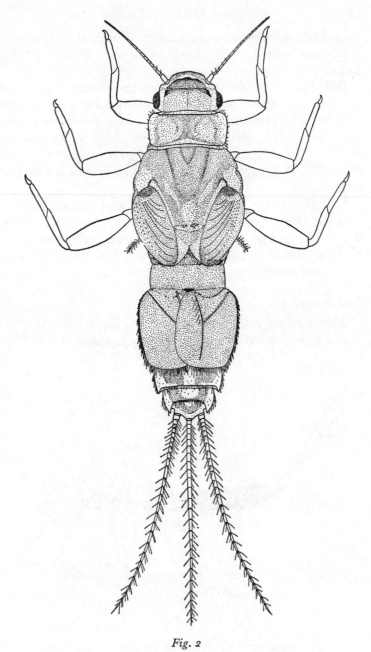

Fig. 2

A silt crawler: the nymph of the River Broadwing (*Caenis macrura*)

East England, and my acquaintance with it is limited to specimens seen in Mr. Alex Behrendt's fishery at Two Lakes near Romsey in Hampshire.

Broadwing nymphs are tiny creatures: the smallest species, *C. rivulorum*, attains an overall length of only about 5.5 mm (.22 inches). They move only slowly and the dense growth of minute hairs which covers their bodies traps particles of fine silt and detritus which serve to conceal the nymphs most effectively in what might otherwise be a rather exposed habitat.

Except perhaps during a flush hatch at sunrise or in the evening, these nymphs are of little significance to the nymph fisherman owing to their unobtrusive habits, which is perhaps just as well as most of them are really too small to imitate effectively.

Moss creepers

These are the rather ponderous, stiff-legged, sturdily built nymphs of the two species of the genus *Ephemerella*. The

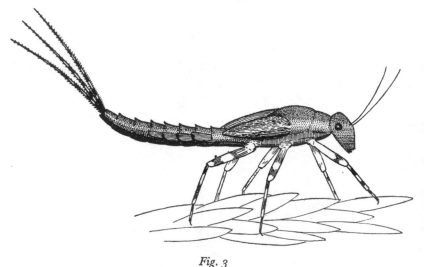

Fig. 3

A moss creeper: the nymph of the Blue-winged Olive
(*Ephemerella ignita*)

nymph of the Blue-winged Olive (*E. ignita*) is common in many parts of the British Isles, occurring in rivers and streams and sometimes in slow-flowing water. Their legs and tails have a characteristic mottled appearance. The nymph of the closely related Yellow Evening dun (*E. notata*) occurs mainly in fast-flowing rivers.

Nymphs of this type creep about, chameleon fashion, among the moss growing on stones on the beds of streams and among weed debris in rivers, especially that trapped along the edges of the stream and in the neighbourhood of bridge piers and hatchways.

I can say little about the Yellow Evening dun for it does not occur regularly in any of the waters which I study. Of the Blue-winged Olive I can say much. It is abundant in flowing water, both fast and slow, in many parts of these islands. The peak emergence period seems to last from mid-June to mid-October, but in 1961 I recorded Blue-winged Olives emerging in every month of the year.

The duns, and hence the nymphs, come in two varieties, large and small, both of which emerge throughout the year. Those which I delivered alive to Mr. Kimmins at the British Museum in February 1961 belonged to the latter category. Within each variety the sexes themselves differ somewhat in size and general appearance.

The nymph of the Blue-winged Olive is therefore a rather inconstant character. As if this weren't enough, it seems to have more trouble than most other species in emerging from the nymph to the dun stage. Its struggles at this time may attract the attention of trout. On some evenings the nymphs have less trouble, so do the nymph fishermen. But occasionally the nymphs experience great difficulty in hatching and any trout which decide to feed selectively on such struggling nymphs are likely, once in a while, to present the nymph fisherman with quite a problem. With patience and care this can sometimes be solved, but if you are in a hurry to catch a fish, I know of only one completely satisfactory solution, namely to find another trout taking duns and to offer it a pheasant-tail Red Spinner!

Stone clingers

A number of different nymphs (*Ecdyonurus, Rhithrogena* and *Heptagenia* spp.) are adapted to cling to stones, boulders and even, in one or two cases, quite smooth pebbles. Such nymphs are capable of maintaining themselves in comparatively unstable conditions of river beds. They have strong legs and their bodies are distinctly flattened to enable them to offer reduced resistance to the current.

Nymphs of the March Brown (*R. haarupi*) are capable of maintaining a hold in fast currents over a stony bed by a process akin to the vacuum suction employed by limpets. They are not easy to displace. Stone clingers are nevertheless able to move quite rapidly over their stony habitat when they wish. Some of the Ecdyonurids are especially quick off the mark, running in a crab-like fashion.

This type of nymph also includes the Olive Upright (*R. semicolorata*), the Dusky Yellowstreak (*H. lateralis*) and the Yellow May dun (*H. sulphurea*), as well as various other Ecdyonurids, none of which are of much significance to the nymph fisherman, in practice.

Nearly all the stone clingers are found in rather fast-flowing water, both rivers and streams, though at least two of them also occur on exposed lake shorelines where, if the bed is stony, wave action can, of course, create relatively unstable conditions. One is the Yellow May dun, a familiar chalk-stream fly and probably the most beautiful of all the upwinged flies. The blue-eyed males seem to be fond of sheltering in apple trees and I often find them in my garden in late May and early June which is their main emergence period. This insect is abundant in the Irish limestone lakes.

The closely related Dusky Yellowstreak (*H. lateralis*), sometimes called the Dark Dun, prefers non-calcareous waters and is especially plentiful in the English Lake District, both along lake shores and in becks, in some of which it is numerous.

1. A Live Natural Nymph.

2. An Artificial Pheasant-Tail Nymph Dressed by the Author.

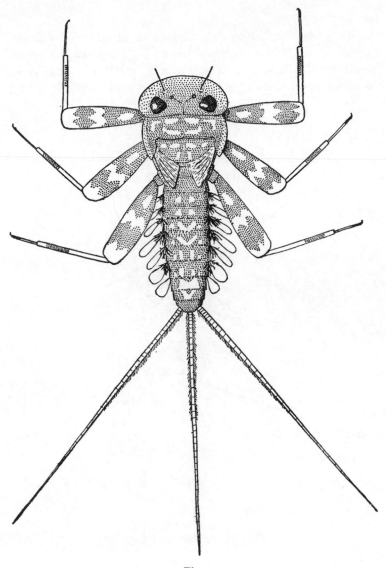

Fig. 4

A stone clinger: the nymph of the Late March Brown
(*Ecdyonurus venosus*)

Laboured swimmers

This group embraces nymphs of a number of related species (*Habrophlebia, Leptophlebia* and *Paraleptophlebia* spp.) found in this country. They spend much of their time crawling about among stones, detritus and weed, for they

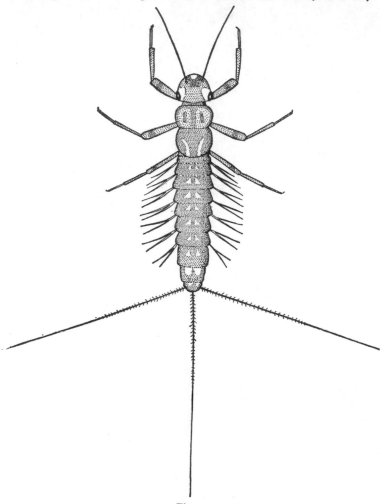

Fig. 5

A laboured swimmer: the nymph of the Turkey Brown
(*Paraleptophlebia submarginata*)

are but poor swimmers though capable of moderate progress through the water when it suits them. Their tails are longer than their bodies, but there are only short ineffectual hairs on each side of each tail filament. These appendages therefore lack the driving power necessary to make them a worthwhile organ of propulsion in the water.

Some of these nymphs develop a protective reddish-brown coloration, especially effective in brown, rather peaty water such as is found in some tarns. The habitat of these species varies quite a lot, however, and with it the effectiveness of the protective coloration.

One of the best-known nymphs of this type is the nymph of the Claret dun (*L. vespertina*) often found in company with the rather similar nymph of the closely related Sepia dun. They both prefer calcareous waters and cannot be distinguished in their early instars. The Sepia dun nymph grows rather more quickly and is therefore the first to emerge, quite early in spring. It has been found at altitudes exceeding 2,500 feet. Despite its preference for peaty water, the nymph of the Claret dun is occasionally recorded in streams of a more alkaline nature, as is the nymph of the little dark three-tailed fly (*H. fusca*), which is still waiting for some sympathetic fisherman-entomologist to give it an English name.

Agile darters

This diverse group includes a few large species (*Siphlonuridae*) which are not often encountered regularly by fly-fishers in this country. They are undoubtedly of importance to those whose fishing takes them to the sub-Arctic lakes of Northern Scandinavia.

Also included in this group are those species which are of the greatest interest and most importance to the nymph fisherman in these islands. They are the nymphs of the Olives, the Iron Blues and the Pale Watery (*Baëtis* spp.), the Spurwings (*Centroplilum* spp.), the Slow and Deep-water Olives (*Cloëon* spp.) and the Pale Evening dun (*P. pseudorufulum*).

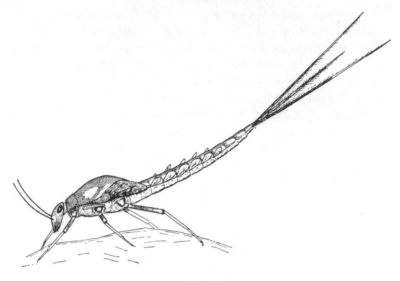

Fig. 6

One of the best-known agile darters: the nymph of the Large Olive
(*Baëtis rhodani*)

All these agile darters are strong swimmers, capable of
rapid movement in the water. They are comparatively
torpedo-shaped and are streamlined, both for speed and
life in flowing water. They all possess remarkably effective
propulsion units in the form of their specially adapted
tails which are about the same length as their bodies.

The median filament of the tail has a dense growth of
hairs or *setae* on each side, thickening perceptibly towards
the tip of the filament. The outer filaments, too, each have
a similar growth of hairs, but only on the inner sides of these
filaments and also thickening towards their tips. Together,
these hair-fringed filaments comprise a tail fin of tremendous
driving power in the water.

Olive (six species), Iron Blue (two species) and Pale
Watery (only one species) nymphs of the genus *Baëtis* occur
only in flowing water, for which alone their respiratory
system fits them. They are all agile, free-ranging, fast swimming nymphs, capable of sudden darting movements. They

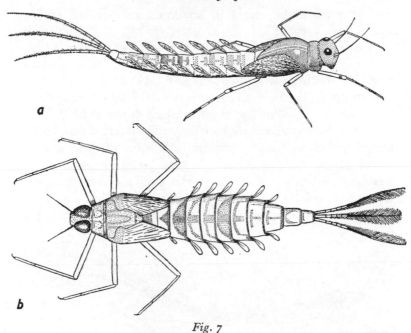

Fig. 7

Two more agile darters: (*a*) the nymph of the Small Spurwing
(*Centroptilum luteolum*); (*b*) the nymph of the Large Spurwing (*C.
pennulatum*)

are all well-known to trout and grayling and also to some
coarse fish, and they figure prominently in the diet of all
these species at times.

Spurwings occur in both fast- and slow-flowing water, but
are found mainly in the latter conditions. They also occur
in some still waters. The Large Spurwing (*C. pennulatum*) is
not a plentiful fly anywhere, to my knowledge. The Small
Spurwing, the nymph of which is probably the most agile
and speedy of all the Ephemeropterans, is one of the most
common anywhere in the country, and is found in a wide
variety of waters.

Cloëon species occur mainly in still waters and can tolerate
comparatively high temperatures. The nymphs of the Slow-
water Olive (*C. dipterum*) are found in both still and slow-
flowing water. In ponds, lakes and reservoirs, it is found

mainly around the edges in shallow, sun-warmed water. It has been recorded in static water tanks and is often seen in garden pools. The closely related Deep-water Olive (*C. simile*) is mainly found in still waters, living among milfoil and other weed at depths of six feet or so.

Nymphs of the Pale Evening dun (*Procloëon pseudorufulum*) occur in the slow-flowing reaches of chalk-streams. I have not, myself, recovered these from still water. Like *Cloëon* nymphs, they are fast swimmers. All three of these species spend much of their time climbing about among water weeds or feeding among weed debris and fallen leaves on the bottom of pools, ponds and so on. When disturbed they dart away with characteristic speed.

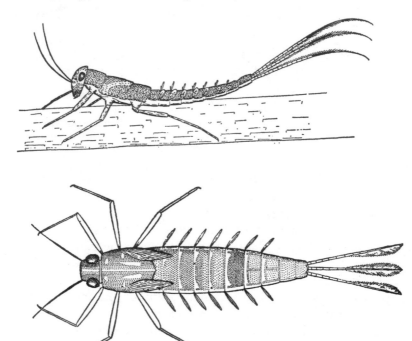

Fig. 8

Further examples of the agile darters: *top*, the nymph of the Slow-water Olive (*Cloëon dipterum*); *bottom*, the nymph of the Pale Evening dun (*Procloëon pseudorufulum*)

The Artificial Nymph

Sinking capability

NATURAL nymphs live under water. That is where artificial nymphs should be fished. The first requirement of an artificial nymph is therefore that it should be constructed to sink. It must penetrate the surface film and sink quite naturally directly it reaches the water. An artificial nymph which will not sink until it becomes waterlogged or unless it has first been anointed with mud or some such preparation as glycerine, is of but limited practical value.

You can carry out a test at home of the suitability of any artificial nymph for fishing purposes. All you need for this is a glass of clean water. Take the dry nymph between finger and thumb and gently release it close to the surface skin of the water. The artificial should penetrate this at once and sink steadily to the bottom of the glass without dithering. Unless the nymph can pass this simple test first time, reject it without hesitation.

Resemblance to the natural nymph

Secondly, if it is to deceive fish, the artificial nymph should bear a reasonable resemblance in structural outline to a natural nymph. As I explained in Chapter One the nymph fisherman is mainly concerned in practice with nymphs of the *Baëtidae* family. Apart from differences in size, which can be reflected in the size of the hook on which the artificial is dressed and, of course, in the amount of dressing applied to it, the natural nymphs of all these species share a common basic structure and are broadly similar in appearance. I therefore use only one pattern of artificial nymph to represent them dressed, of course, on hooks of various sizes from oo to 1.

The natural nymph is characterized by a small head, humped thorax which includes the wing cases, slender tapering abdomen, and tails. The artificial nymph, likewise, should have a small head, a humped thorax, tapering abdomen, and tails. Whatever dressing is employed to create such an artificial must also meet the first specification of incorporating a quick-sinking capability.

Sawyer uses gossamer-fine copper wire as the tying medium for his nymph. No silk is used in the construction. The wire is wound on to the bare hook in such a way as to build up the structural outline of the artificial. This wire also serves to weight the hook and gives the nymph its requisite quick-sinking capability.

Nymphs required for fishing in still water, especially shallow still water, call for the incorporation of less wire in their construction than those intended for employment in fast-flowing streams and in the deep pools of rivers.

Obtaining wire of the requisite gossamer fineness presents something of a problem. I have never been able to buy it at fishing-tackle shops. Wireless repair shops are sometimes a promising draw, for spools of fine copper wire feature in the make-up of wireless transformers and unserviceable sets in the "back rooms" can sometimes be cannibalised to provide supplies.

Over the wire foundation on the hook is superimposed a simple dressing of herls. I prefer herls from the long middle tail feather of an old cock pheasant, but the blue herls from a heron primary or the grey herls from a goose are also effective. When I dress a small nymph on a size oo hook I do not use more than three herls. For a larger nymph on a size 1 hook, I use as many as five.

The ends of the herls are fastened down with a couple of turns of wire so that they project to serve as the nymph's tails. They should not be longer than ⅜ in. or they will suggest a hook with trailing weed rather than a natural nymph with tails. The main part of the herls is then carefully wound on the abdomen, beginning at the tail end and ending at the shoulder. When wound round the shank of the hook to make the abdomen of the artificial nymph, the fibres of the pheasant-tail herls stand out, suggesting the tracheal gills in a most realistic way. After the wound herls have completely covered the body of the nymph, the remnant should be doubled and re-doubled at the dorsal thorax to form the thorax and suggest the wing cases. Finally all should be made fast behind the eye with a couple of turns and two half hitches. The nymph is then ready for service.

The aim of putting any kind of dressing on to the hook during the construction of a nymph should be to make the artificial look like a natural nymph without in any way prejudicing its free-sinking capability. Both requirements suggest that it should not be encumbered with hackle, streamers or other such superfluous attachments. It is true enough that large-hackled lures, commonly referred to as "nymphs", do catch fish, especially in reservoirs. They do so quite simply because the fish take them in mistake for food, food of a variety of kinds. But they are not really representations of nymphs nor, I suggest, do fish accept them as nymphs. This in no way detracts from the usefulness of hackled lures, especially to the reservoir fisherman. The same may be said of effective non-hackled lures.

No normal reservoir trout feeding on sticklebacks or other relatively substantial aquatic food creatures can be expected to go out of its way to take a tiny nymph, either natural or artificial, though if it happens to swim almost into direct contact with the nymph, it may well accept it, in passing. Exactly the same may be said of chalk-stream trout when they are minnowing in summer.

Once in a while, when the duns of some still-water up-winged species are emerging in great numbers, still-water trout feed readily enough on the natural nymphs. In these circumstances they may be taken quite effectively on the

type of artificial nymph which I use and have described
above. But even on these occasions they may accept lures
like Mr. Ivens's Black Spider, dressed on a much larger hook
than I use. A hungry trout would be stupid to pass up the
opportunity of an easy mouthful.

It is possible that substantial lures, both hackled "nymph"
and non-hackled "bug" patterns, would be as effective or
even more effective in the chalk-streams than the type of
artificial nymph which I employ. On many waters, however,
their use would not conform to the rules of the fishery so the
question remains largely hypothetical. The chalk-streams
especially have a narrow but generally accepted concept of
what constitutes an artificial nymph, except that lightly
hackled nymphs are allowed on some but prohibited on
others. My own view is that an artificial nymph is a reasonably close representation in size and general appearance of a
natural nymph. I have not yet seen a natural nymph with
wings. Winged artificials may be effective, indeed we know
they are, but they are not nymphs. They may be conveniently thought of and fairly described as wet flies. With
regard to hackled nymphs, if the rules of the water permit
the use of hackled nymphs, it is up to the individual to
employ these patterns if he so wishes.

To revert to the herls used in nymph dressing, these help
to give the artificial a more finished and pleasing appearance
to the human eye. I find that in practice I continue to
catch fish, both trout and grayling, on my wired hooks long
after the herls have worn away through hard usage, provided that the basic structural outline with its humped thorax
remains.

Hooking power

The third and final requirement of the artificial nymph is that it must be capable of hooking and holding fish effectively. This calls for good-quality hooks with sharp, penetrative points, efficient barbs, strong shanks and sound eyes. Every consignment of hooks which reaches me from my suppliers includes some which visibly fall short of this standard. These I reject. In general it is fair to say that the quality of our hooks leaves much to be desired, to put it mildly.

As for the best type of hook for dressing artificial nymphs, I think this is largely a matter of individual preference. I have tied nymphs on and caught fish with most of the standard types of hook, yet I always prefer down-eyed Limerick hooks on which it so happens that the first nymphs I used had been dressed and it is on these that the great majority of my fish have since been taken.

Although an artificial nymph may continue to deceive fish long after much of the dressing has worn away, it will only go on hooking them effectively if the point is kept sharp. If a nymph ever shows signs of rust or its barb becomes damaged in any way, I scrap it. The use of suspect nymphs is folly for which there is little excuse. Most of us have learned this lesson the hard way, and I am no exception.

As artificial nymphs are fished in the water, they get wet. When you remove a wet nymph from the point of your cast, be careful not to introduce moisture anywhere where it may lead to rusting or deterioration of your stock.

PATTERNS NECESSARY

The pattern of an artificial nymph and the precise method of its construction is inevitably influenced by individual preference and personal experience in practice. No doubt there is pleasure to be had from dressing nymphs in different ways, especially when· experimenting with new or unusual materials. Do not lose sight of the fact that the effectiveness

of an artificial nymph depends not on how it appeals to us
but on its appeal to the fish. I have described the type of
nymph I use because I know that its effectiveness has been
thoroughly tested and established. If you have a pattern of
some other kind which you yourself find effective, stick to
it. But if you have had trouble in finding a nymph pattern
which will work, try the one I use.

If you were offered a helping of the sharp but otherwise
worn, threadbare and disreputable-looking nymphs from my
box, you would probably decline, wondering however I
manage to catch fish on them at all. Presently I hope to
tell you.

Always remember that the appeal of a nymph to a fish is
only partly dependent on its superficial external appearance.
It is much more important that the artificial should be fished
in such a way as to appear to be behaving like a natural
nymph in the water. *Successful nymph fishing is primarily
dependent on the life-like employment of the artificial by the angler.*
The practical aspects of fishing the artificial nymph will be
dealt with in later chapters.

I appreciate that some fly-fishers may prefer to try to
relate the appearance of their artificial nymph to the natural
nymph on which they suppose a trout to be mainly feeding
when they cast to it. This approach may add to the interest
of nymph fishing, just as the employment of a variety of
different patterns adds interest to dry-fly fishing. There are
times, however, when even the most reliable dry-fly patterns
fail to induce trout to take, however carefully presented. I
have experienced no such difficulty with regard to the
artificial nymph I employ, except that sometimes I have
been obliged to use a slightly smaller pattern to be sure of
trout taking confidently.

To deduce which species of nymph a fish may be taking
when feeding under water is not at all easy. The assumption
that it is probably the nymph of the fly on the water rarely
bears close examination. Indeed fly-fishers are apt to overlook the fact that daytime hatches of duns are rarely confined to one species, or even two or three.

As early as 15th January, 1961, I recorded a mixed hatch of Blue-winged Olives and Olives at Netheravon and on the same day recovered live male Small Spurwing and Dark Olive duns. Early in the grayling season the hatch on October 13th yielded me Blue-winged Olives, Olives, Small Olives, Pale Watery duns, Small Spurwings, Iron Blues (*B. niger*) and Large Olives, in that order of abundance. Next day I collected Blue-winged Olives, Olives, Small Olives, Dark Olives, Iron Blues (*B. pumilus*) and Small Spurwings. Who was to say which of these species were being taken, as nymphs, by the grayling? I doubt very much whether the fish are greatly concerned to distinguish between these nymphs except, perhaps, on a basis of size.

In my experience it is unnecessary to carry more than one pattern of artificial nymph dressed, of course, in several sizes with variable sinking capability, according to the water to be fished. There are obvious advantages in carrying an additional pattern, especially to employ as a change if a chance is muffed on the basic pattern. There are, however, other ways of redeeming missed chances. But again the individual nymph fisherman is at liberty to please himself. If you feel you need three different patterns, my advice to you would be to use three. I shall continue to use one for the very sound reason that so far, wherever I have fished, I have only found one necessary. When I find I need another, I shan't hesitate to dress one. Until then, there is no point in me recommending patterns for which I can foresee no requirement.

Always, throughout the year, I carry a small box in the boot of my car containing a reel of fine copper wire, some pheasant tail feathers, a few cock's necks, a tin of silks, a few heron, goose and rook primaries, some peacock herls, a vice, a hackle pliers, a razor blade, a dubbing needle, a box of miscellaneous feathers and another of dubbing furs. All the fish I catch are caught on flies and nymphs which I tie myself from this simple outfit.

The effectiveness of my one artificial nymph in actual practice is clearly apparent from the following statistics relating to my total catch of fish on fly during the five successive seasons, 1957–61:

Artificial	Trout	Grayling	Coarse Fish	Total
Nymph	551	1,176	33	1,760
Red Spinner	128	141	2	271
Olive Dun	102	92	—	194
Hawthorn-fly	58	18	1	77
Iron Blue	12	43	—	55
Mayfly	30	19	—	49
Kite's Sedge	25	11	—	36
All others	45	15	1	61
	951	1,515	37	2,503

These figures show that this one nymph pattern accounted for an average of 352 fish a year out of a total average annual basket of 500. This amounts to more than 70% of all the fish I catch. There is, I suggest, not much wrong with a pattern capable of yielding such a result consistently, year after year.

★ 3 ★

When to Fish the Nymph

THE STATUS OF NYMPH FISHING

I N SOME waters, in some parts of the country, at certain
times of the year, natural nymphs constitute a high proportion of the aquatic food creatures which feature in
the diet of trout, grayling and some other fish. When a
trout or grayling is actively feeding on nymphs in preference
to hatched fly, the employment of an artificial nymph to
catch such a fish is then no more than logical, always providing that nymph fishing is permissible according to the
rules of the water.

It might be as well to make clear at this stage that certain
fisheries, both river and lake, restrict the use of the artificial
nymph. Its employment may be barred during the early
months of the season, perhaps until July 1st or thereabouts.
There are even a few fisheries where nymph fishing is prohibited altogether and only the dry-fly is allowed. Some
private owners, too, prefer to maintain a "dry-fly only"
tradition. Obviously a visitor will stick to the rules and a
guest will be careful to fall in with his host's wishes in this
matter. It is therefore always advisable to make certain what
these are, if you are visiting private water, before you begin
to fish. If for any reason you have been unable to do this,
it might be as well not to risk abusing hospitality or infringing
the rules by nymph fishing. Stick to the dry-fly until you
can be sure how you stand.

The question of whether to use the nymph or the dry-fly
when the rules permit the employment of both is best decided
by observation. When you see a trout feeding under water,

turning and lifting repeatedly to intercept nymphs and other sub-aqueous food creatures, the prospects of inducing it to rise to a dry-fly fished on the surface may not be at all good. If you care to use your eyes, you should be able to determine what these prospects are by observing this particular fish's behaviour. If you see it take any natural dun, spinner, or dipteran floating over it, it is reasonable to expect it to rise to a nicely presented dry-fly. As dry-fly fishing is a comparatively easy way of catching a trout, the employment of this method to take such a fish has much to recommend it.

If the trout visibly ignores occasional natural flies on the surface but continues to feed freely under water, it is unreasonable to expect it to rise to the surface to take an artificial dry-fly. It is not only unreasonable, to my way of thinking it is also unethical. This is not too strong a description for the pointless and unnecessary pestering of a trout, a living creature, which this would amount to.

To harry a trout with dry-flies when it is feeding underwater, and only underwater, simply adds to the fish's education, making it more and more familiar with the appearance and behaviour of artificial dry-flies. In time this educating process makes it more and more difficult to induce such a trout to rise to an artificial dry-fly on the surface.

The fact that duns may be seen hatching in good numbers and that fish are apparently moving well does not always necessarily imply that these fish are feeding on the duns. In some circumstances, indeed, it is quite probable that they are taking the mature nymphs shortly before they emerge as duns.

During the summer months the wings of those duns which commonly hatch by day at that time, especially Pale Wateries and Small Spurwings, dry so quickly in the sunshine that the flies are able to leave the water almost as soon as they emerge, giving trout little time to take them. In these circumstances it is not unusual to find trout moving freely during a hatch of these duns, showing rise forms breaking the surface, but with the fish in fact taking nymphs just beneath it. Use your eyes, always, in fly-fishing, whether

3. Haxton Bridge over the Avon near the Author's Cottage.

4. Wing Commander Anthony Coke Fishing his Water on the Wylye near Heytesbury.

with dry-fly or nymph. Your eyes, indeed, should tell you which to employ.

Fish sometimes take duns and nymphs impartially, more especially if conditions are moist and the duns' wings dry more slowly. They then sit a little longer on their shucks and trout, finding them easier to catch, accept them more readily.

Wind may also influence trout to feed under water during a hatch of duns. A light downstream wind is usually conducive to good sport with the dry-fly, given the presence of hatched fly on the water. Even a strong downstream wind is not wholly inimical to dry-fly fishing if the difficulties of casting in these conditions can be overcome. But whereas a downstream wind presses flies, both natural and artificial, on the waiting trout, a strong upstream wind has the reverse effect, blowing surface fly away from them and causing them much frustration. In these circumstances I have often known trout give up the attempt to feed on the surface during a substantial hatch of duns. Remember, however, that few rivers flow straight and bad conditions on one reach may be quite favourable on another round the next bend.

The practical fly-fisher is surely one who arrives at the waterside without preconceived notions of fishing either the nymph or the dry-fly but capable of employing effectively whichever one of them is appropriate to the situation which exists on the day, and from time to time during the day.

The nymph and the dry-fly should not be adjudged superior or inferior one to another. It all depends on the circumstances prevailing at any given time. The two should always be regarded as complementary to each other.

In actual practice, the relative number of trout taken by me on nymph and dry-fly, fishing regularly throughout the past five seasons, have been:

	1957	*1958*	*1959*	*1960*	*1961*	*Totals*
Nymph	85	160	62	120	124	551
Dry-fly	43	76	41	79	161	400
	128	236	103	199	285	951

These figures show clearly enough that either the nymph or the dry-fly may take most trout during the course of the season, though it is significant that in four of these five seasons the nymph proved more rewarding than the dry-fly. I daresay, too, that if you cared to count their stomach contents, you would find more nymphs than hatched flies in four out of every five trout you catch, if you can catch them throughout the season.

THE MONTHS WHEN THE NYMPH SCORES

I have analysed the figures summarised on page 49 (table) in considerable detail. They show that the dry-fly is altogether more effective than the nymph during the early months of the season but that by mid-summer it is overtaken by the nymph which throughout July and August accounts for a high proportion of all trout caught. The great majority of fish taken by me during the daytime in these months were caught on the artificial nymph. By September, when the summer generation of nymphs emerge, the dry-fly comes back into its own and, incidentally, provides good sport during the early part of the grayling season until about the end of October. Thereafter the grayling fisher is likely to find the nymph more profitable (see Chapter Fifteen).

As a practical illustration of the typical pattern of a chalk-stream fly-fishing season, the monthly breakdown of the trout I caught on the Upper Avon in 1961 discloses the following summary of fish taken on the various patterns I employed:

May: Hawthorn fly, 14; Olive Dun, 5; Mayfly, 3; Red Spinner, 1; Iron Blue, 1; Black Gnat, 1; total 25.

June: Pale Watery Dun, 4; Pale Evening Dun, 4; Red Spinner, 3; Nymph, 2; total 13.

July: Nymph, 16; Pale Evening Dun, 2; Red Spinner, 1; total 19.

August: Nymph, 13; Red Spinner, 10; total 23.

September: Red Spinner, 13; Nymph, 7; Iron Blue, 1; total 21.

1961 totals: Nymph 38, Red Spinner 28, Hawthorn-fly 14,

Pale Evening Dun 6, Olive Dun 5, Pale Watery Dun 4, Mayfly 3, Iron Blue 2, and Black Gnat 1; total for Upper Avon, 101.

My half-rod entitles me to fish one day a week on this water where the daily limit is three brace. Fishing most weeks it is theoretically possible to catch about 120 trout a season. In practice, the five seasons 1957–61 inclusive yielded me 502 trout from this water so the 1961 total may fairly be regarded as typical.

The above monthly breakdown clearly reflects the early excitements of the Hawthorn-fly at the beginning of May, when Black Gnats may also be on the water, over-shadowing the early hatches of Olives and Iron Blues; the Mayfly interlude, followed by the appearance of Pale Wateries during the day in June and Pale Evening duns on hot evenings after mid-summer; the dominance of the nymph throughout the daytime in July and for much of August; and the re-establishment of dry-fly ascendancy in September.

I did not use the artificial nymph on the Upper Avon in 1961 until June 24th. We generally think of June as the start of the nymph-fishing season but it is in peak demand during the day-time in July and August.

NOT EVERYONE'S CHOICE

I do not recommend that every fly-fisher should use the artificial nymph. There are at least two good reasons why I refrain from making any such suggestion.

In the first place, every fly-fisher is entitled to decide for himself how he will attempt to catch his fish within the rules, and the spirit of the rules, of the water he fishes. Now it is a fact that many fly-fishers find their chief pleasure in catching trout on the dry-fly. Although I get keen personal enjoyment from my nymph fishing, there are times when I feel this way myself.

For me the cream of the chalk-stream trout season comes right at the beginning when the Hawthorn-fly is on the water, often in quite testing conditions of sun and wind, and good trout are rising freely to the artificial which, year in and year out, yields me two or three times as many fish as the Mayfly—I am speaking of the post-1956 period and not of the Edwardian era.

If I go to the river late on a summer evening after a long and perhaps rather exhausting day, and I see the Blue-winged Olive hatching in quantities and observe against the reflected afterglow that trout are taking the duns of this species, I relax in the comforting expectation of rewarding sport on the dry-fly. No great effort of concentration or co-ordination is required to catch trout feeding on Blue-winged Olives, and one can fish the pheasant tail Red Spinner on these occasions just for pleasure and still be reasonably sure of catching trout with the minimum of tension and strain.

On such evenings as these, I may see other fish taking the Blue-winged Olive nymph. If I am fishing for pleasure I leave them to enjoy it in peace. If I am looking for a challenge, I have found it, for here is one capable of testing any fly-fisher at times.

It is, I think, a great mistake to lose the capacity for fly-fishing for pleasure. Nymph fishing, to be effective, is a very exacting form of fly-fishing, infinitely more exacting than the dry-fly. If for this reason a man prefers to fish solely with the dry-fly, there is no reason why he should not succeed in catching a reasonable share of fish, always provided that he offers the dry-fly to fish he sees feeding on the surface. Indeed, I always encourage pupils to master the dry-fly before they take up serious nymph fishing. Dry-fly fishing, after all, is fishing in two dimensions, and to that extent alone is much easier than nymph fishing which embraces three dimensions.

It is a fascinating and most instructive experience to take a class of 40 or 50 fly-fishers out to fish the evening rise on a big chalk-stream. Those who attend my Salisbury classes are for the most part seasoned fishermen from the counties round about. Many have rods on the major chalk-streams and such other well-known still-water fisheries as Two Lakes. They include riparian owners and their keepers, members of syndicates and, sometimes, a leavening of apprentices. And there are some very good lady fly-fishers among them each year.

Many of them throw a fly extremely well, having taken lessons from leading professional casting instructors before they ever come to me to learn the practical application of the art of fly-fishing. Accordingly, when they present a fly or nymph to a trout and the fish refuses their offer several times running, they first of all want to know why. Then, having heard my diagnosis, they often ask me to try to catch the fish myself to prove my theoretical explanation. Before I cast, I try to forecast how I expect the trout to react to my offer and, in nymph fishing, to explain my intentions if I propose to induce some particular reaction by the fish.

Although the primary aim of a fly-fishing instructor is to teach his pupil how to catch fish, to be of any practical value the instruction must necessarily leave the pupil in no doubt as to why and in just what circumstances certain methods and actions generally prove successful and others usually fail. One of the first and most important lessons to inculcate in practical fly-fishing instruction is the value of observation. This brings me to the second good reason why some fly-fishers cannot be expected to do well with the nymph. I refer to indifferent or failing sight.

Good eyesight is an invaluable though not indispensable asset of the dry-fly fisherman. It is, I believe, absolutely essential for the nymph fisherman. It is not difficult to prove this contention. Get a friend to go with you to a river you know well, assemble your tackle for fishing wet with one or more flies, allow yourself to be effectively blindfolded, then fish across and down. If you have a feel for water, as most experienced fly-fishers have, you don't need a particularly keen sense of touch to discern the plucks of fish which take your fly or flies and you hook quite a few despite the un-accustomed limitation of artificial blindness. But try the same experiment fishing a nymph upstream when you are blindfolded. Unless you are very lucky or have practised this blindfold technique thoroughly, you not only don't hook any fish, you don't even realize when fish take and eject your nymph. It is illuminating to all present if you conduct the experiment accompanied by one who knows the form and can give you a running commentary on what is taking place. I am speaking of experiments conducted with wild trout. Stock fish behave quite differently, especially the bigger trout during the first weeks after they are turned into a river or lake (see Chapter Ten).

SOME PERSONAL RESERVATIONS

Hook sizes

I have certain reservations about nymph fishing in practice which, let me make it quite clear, I regard as of purely personal application. I do not, for example, employ nymphs dressed on hooks larger than size 1. Indeed, except for fishing for trout in very fast water on rough rivers or for grayling fishing in deep pools in autumn and winter, I rarely carry let alone use nymphs larger than size o. Larger artificials can be very effective. To deny this would be both stupid and unrealistic. But I think of them as lures, mistaken by trout for food creatures other than natural nymphs. So I do not use them. Every man is entitled to his own idiosyncracies and to determine his own standards of conduct in practice, provided always that he does not try to impose them on others.

Mayfly nymphs

Trout eat Mayfly nymphs, and relish them, as they ascend from their burrows to emerge on the surface as Mayflies. Trout also eat these Mayfly subimagines on the surface. When they do, I fish for them with a dry hackled mink-bodied Mayfly. If I can't catch them with this, I give them best although I know that there are days when trout taking the natural Mayfly can be damnably difficult. The point is they do take it and for me, personally, deceiving them then is part of the challenge. In such circumstances it would be spiritual prostitution for me to put on a nymph on a No. 5

hook and use this to butcher trout with. For this is what using a large Mayfly nymph amounts to, in my opinion.

The heart of the matter

The question the nymph fisherman should ask himself is simply this. What is he trying to do? If he merely wants to take fish, he would do better, I suggest, to use a net or borrow an electric fishing apparatus.

If he wants to catch trout on rod and line, let him use worms or maggots or minnows, or Hare's Ears, or whatever else the rules of the water he is fishing allow him to use. His aim is quite straightforward and these methods are calculated to serve his ends legitimately in these circumstances. Anyone motivated by a desire to prevent fish being caught should be honest and join some society seeking to abolish the sport of angling, though they will get no help from me. But if our nymph fisherman wants to deceive trout, grayling and, perhaps, coarse fish with an imitation of a *nymph* when they are feeding under water, let him decide for himself what constitutes a *nymph*. He is free then to formulate his own concept of *nymph fishing*, within the spirit of the rules of the water he fishes, subject to such personal reservations as he deems appropriate, and having regard both to the circumstances and to his own standard of performance.

I have confined myself here to an expression of my own feelings about nymph fishing and I do not wish to show or imply any disrespect for others who may feel differently. But let us be clear that from here on, it is with the Netheravon conception of an artificial nymph and the Netheravon style of nymph fishing that I shall be dealing.

★ 4 ★

Tackle for Nymph Fishing

The important factors

TACKLE for nymph fishing is basically much the same as that required for dry-fly fishing. This is a matter of some convenience since a fly-fisher may wish to employ both methods from time to time during the course of a day's fishing, according to whichever is appropriate to the situation at any given moment. Not all fly-fishers can, in any case, afford to equip themselves with alternative outfits for dry-fly and nymph fishing, even if these were desirable.

There are, however, certain factors which the nymph fisherman should take into account when choosing his tackle, if it is not too late for him to do so. The first important requirement is to be able to present the artificial nymph at the level at which the fish is feeding—nymph fishing being three-dimensional fly-fishing—and the second is to be able to deal effectively with the fish when it accepts the artificial by which it has been deceived. This means hooking it.

Presentation necessitates pitching the nymph into the water lightly but accurately at such a distance from the fish's lie as will enable it to sink to a point close to the head of the fish by the time it reaches it. Clearly, a fine cast point is essential for this purpose otherwise the nymph will be prevented from sinking quickly. Moreover, unless the water is uniformly shallow, this fine point must be reasonably long to permit effective sinking to the required depth. This

56

in turn affects the composition of the rest of the cast. Casts
for nymph fishing will be discussed in greater detail later in
this chapter.

Striking and hooking depend partly on the suitability of
the rod to initiate the strike, the lightness of the line to
enable it to be instantly effective, and, of course, the quality
and sharpness of the hooks employed in dressing the artificials used.

The line

In practice it is a good deal easier to put a fly a long way
into a wind with a heavy line, and a rod designed to throw
it, than with a light line and a rod of appropriate strength.
But trout take and eject an artificial dry-fly much more
slowly than they take and eject a nymph. There is nothing
leisurely about the take of an artificial nymph most times,
nor is there any delay in ejecting it again when the deception
is discovered.

To be effective, therefore, a strike must be made very
quickly, for the hook must be driven home during the brief
moment when the fish closes its mouth on the nymph.
Unless the tackle permits of this being done, it will not be
satisfactory for nymph fishing, however serviceable it may
have proved to be in practice with the dry-fly. This is not
to say that expensive, stiffish, split-cane rods and No. 4 lines
will not catch trout on the artificial nymph. They will,
particularly if you have had a certain amount of experience
to accustom yourself to handling them to the best advantage,
but by using them for nymph fishing, I think that you
handicap yourself considerably.

Ideally, a No. 1 line should be used for nymph fishing,
with a rod of appropriate capability. If you can afford
several sets of tackle, and if you expect to do a fair amount
of daytime nymph fishing in the summer months, it is indeed
convenient to have an outfit expressly designed for this
purpose. I own no such tackle myself nor have I felt the
need of it, but I have handled some superb nymph-fishing
rods and light lines belonging to my friends.

Tackle made for nymph fishing, good quality equipment, makes this rather difficult and exacting sport that much easier in practice. I would suggest, however, that if you own a No. 2 line and a rod and reel well matched to it, you should not find trout unduly difficult to hook on the nymph. The most expensive tackle ever devised isn't going to turn a ham-fisted fly-fisher into a master and, equally, a man who calls himself a nymph fisherman ought to be able to take trout on a nymph on any reasonable combination of fly-fishing tackle. But don't go out of your way to make difficulties for yourself.

I use a double-tapered line and used to be able to make a line last two seasons, beginning each with a different end. But although I hardly use an inch off the end of a line during the course of a full season, the line itself becomes so frayed and cracked from constant handling in wet conditions that I don't get much more than one season's wear out of a line nowadays. It all depends how much use a line is put to. Including grayling fishing, I use my fly lines about 80 days a year.

The rod

I have caught trout on an artificial nymph using rods made of many different materials: split cane, greenheart, fibre glass and steel. Rods of every length from six feet to 14. The disadvantages of greenheart are well known. My experiences with steel rods have been unfortunate. One broke at the ferrule and the top joint, carrying away the cast, shot out into the river never to be seen again. The next steel rod I used was a short seven-footer. It threw a nymph well enough but after a couple of hours casting in a high wind fractured some distance from the terminal ring of the top joint. The line touched no obstruction and I can only conclude that the rod had developed metal fatigue. To be absolutely fair, some of my friends have a good opinion of steel rods, but they are not nymph fishermen.

For several years I used nothing but split cane rods and I have caught many hundreds of trout and grayling on the nymph on a No. 2 line and a rod of about eight feet six inches for which I paid eight guineas. It is still as good as ever.

In 1961 I used Milbrolite fibre glass rods extensively for both nymph and dry-fly fishing and I have never enjoyed a better season. I am content to use most of the comparatively few rods I own for both nymph and dry-fly fishing impartially. I always take at least two rods with me when I go fishing in case I am unfortunate enough to damage one of them during the course of the day. It is a profoundly irritating experience to travel a long distance to fish some far-off river and then to have to come back again for reserve tackle in the event of an accident.

Rods which suit one man may not appeal to another. My advice to anyone thinking of buying a rod for nymph fishing would be to get in touch with a reliable dealer who is himself a nymph fisherman or with one of the firms, and there are several in this country today, whose executives are well known both for their casting skill and practical fishing experience.

Do be warned, however, that some who sell fishing tackle have an imperfect understanding of nymph fishing which they tend to confuse with wet-fly fishing. I have a wet-fly rod with a delightfully sweet action which I treasure very much. It is ideal for the purpose for which it was designed. But for nymph fishing on the exposed rivers of Salisbury Plain it is almost useless.

To recapitulate then, the rod must be suited to the line which is the controlling item in the choice of tackle. It must be capable of instant and effective striking, and it must be able to stand up to sustained hard work in windy weather.

The cast

I recommend at least three feet of fine nylon on the point of the cast. I say nylon because I gave up using gut in 1957. Up to that time nylon had not seemed altogether reliable, but since I made the change I have not once had cause to doubt its suitability for fly-fishing. I make all my own casts, for this is the most convenient way of having them according to the specification which I find suits my style best. This is probably cheaper than buying casts, as well, but this is only incidental.

For nymph fishing with a rod about eight feet six inches to nine feet long, I like a cast between nine and ten feet in length. Using a tapered line, the cast must be graduated from a butt which is almost as thick as the end of the line to the fine nylon on the point. I use nylon of about five different thicknesses to make up such a cast, joining the strands with a triple blood knot. I like the thick butt to be about half the total length of the cast, say about four feet six inches, and use a blood bight to make the loop for attaching the end of the tapered line. With three intermediate sections each of about ten inches and three feet on the point this makes up a cast with a total length of ten feet.

A typical detailed specification for a nylon cast for nymph fishing is:

4 ft. 6 in. of ·016 in., 10 in. of ·012 in., 10 in. of ·009 in., 10 in. of ·008 in. and 3 ft. of ·007 in.

Using continental nylon, I make up my normal cast as follows:

1·50 metres of 0·40 m., 0·25 m. of 0·32 mm., 0·25 m. of 0·24 mm., 0·25 m. of 0·18 mm. and 1·00 m. of 0·16 mm.

I don't say that these specifications are not capable of improvement, theoretically. They may be. But these are the casts I use for catching fish and intend to go on using until someone produces an alternative which I, not he, find more effective in nymph-fishing practice.

In practice, breakages occur from time to time, especially when fishing during windy weather in the presence of rank bankside vegetation or many willows or other trees. When I am out fishing, therefore, I carry a thin flat plastic reel of fine point nylon in the inside pocket of my old green fishing jacket or in the left breast pocket of my dark green waterproof jacket, if the day is wet. These spare spools are kept permanently in the respective coat pockets and are replaced whenever they show signs of running low. I likewise permanently carry a small red tin of mucilin in a separate pocket in each coat for greasing the thicker parts of my cast when fishing in reflected light, bad visibility or rough water.

I am told that there is little to choose between most types of nylon as far as quality is concerned. As regards strength this may be true but some kinds seem to me to be decidedly more manageable than others. Where nylon is concerned I greatly dislike any tendency to wiriness or curling. I like a docile nylon, and when I can get it, I always use Luron. I have also bought some good plain nylon in Bavaria. I brought back some beautifully camouflaged fine nylon which I bought on the Left Bank in Paris, but it took the eye of my friends and I hadn't enough experience with it to enable me to decide whether there were any advantages in using it or not. For myself I don't really mind what colour the various strands of my cast are, although I normally buy a clear greenish-tinged nylon for preference. In Salisbury I find I usually have to take what I can get!

If a point has caught up in bankside vegetation and curled round on itself several times, causing it to kink after being unwound, I get rid of it and tie on another. I use the treble blood knot for all my knots at the waterside, biting off the spare ends with my teeth after pulling them tight. I am averse to carrying an ounce of unnecessary weight and as long as I have my front teeth I shall consider scissors to be in this category.

SOME PRACTICAL TIPS

De-greasing the cast

A cast can easily become affected by grease, either through contact with line floatant or fly oil or through being handled with fingers smeared with these substances or butter, fat and so on from the lunch basket. This has serious consequences when nymph fishing because the artificial is prevented from sinking freely to the level at which the fish is feeding. If necessary the point must be de-greased from time to time to ensure retention of a good sinking capability.

The best natural cure for a greasy cast is undoubtedly mud, soft mud, but this may not be easy to find if the weather has been dry and the banks are of sand, gravel or chalk. Sand itself will clean a cast very well but it will also fray and weaken it and is not to be recommended for fine points. Gentler alternatives should be sought.

Young dock leaves bruise easily and when folded make a useful damp pad for wiping down a cast to de-grease it. If dock leaves are not available, many others may be used in a similar way, but be chary of picking rather large and vaguely rhubarb-like leaves, some of which are coated with spiny hairs which can be painfully irritating if they pierce the skin.

Some saddle fungus can also be used. It is commonly found growing on the trunks of waterside trees, especially birches and old willows, from which a piece of convenient size may be broken off. The cast will slice into the moist fungus which is then squeezed gently round it while the nylon is being drawn gently through to clean it.

Useful sinking agents, so essential when nymph fishing, include saliva, blood from the gills of trout already killed, mucus from grayling, and worm casts. Wet clay is even more effective and not so unpleasant to handle. The most convenient place to look or feel for it is against the edge of the heel under the instep of one boot. Only if the banks are very dry is this source likely to be unrewarding.

It is usually possible to find mud even in drought conditions in the chalk country, if you know where to look for it. If there are trees nearby, look for leaf mould in adjacent hollows, particularly if they are beeches or hawthorns. In the open there are generally moist patches under large stones, baulks of timber or fallen branches, especially in hollows.

Remember too that many plants which grow at the water's edge create their own soil bed by filtering fine mud particles from the current. The chances are that watercress, for example, will be harbouring soft black mud at its roots even when it is growing in the bright gravel bed of a clear chalk stream. No gentler substance can be found for de-greasing a fine 4x point.

Carrying your nymphs

Do not carry nymphs in a fly box. If you do, you will inevitably introduce damp and this moisture will lead to rusting and general deterioration of your dry flies. Have a separate box for your nymphs and let it be small, convenient for the pocket, and easy to keep a firm hold of when you are standing shivering on an unstable bottom in rough water with a strained wrist on a cold windy day.

Right from the start I have carried my nymphs in a little round plastic box given to me by my wife. I believe it once held face cream of some kind. The lid has a rough serrated edge and there is no danger of losing a grip on it. Its diameter is no greater than that of half a crown. But every year when I go to the Game Fair, it holds seven dozen new nymphs and when I come back it is usually almost empty. Some people reading these lines now may recall this little box and remember helping themselves, at my invitation, to a pinch of nymphs from it as men once accepted a pinch of snuff.

Marrow scoops and all that

One or two of my friends are the proud owners of an old-fashioned marrow scoop which, as every fly-fisher knows, is a useful aid for determining just what trout were feeding on at the time of their capture.

Useful as they undoubtedly are, marrow scoops are nowadays very difficult to obtain. Since you rarely see or hear of them being used for the purpose for which they were originally intended, this may require some explanation. The fact is that marrow scoops, like old-fashioned motor cars and many other antique things, are much sought after by collectors for their own sake, ending up in display cases up and down the country and thereby being lost to enquiring and deserving fly-fishers, perhaps for good.

I have never been fortunate enough to own a marrow scoop myself, but for some years I managed quite well with a long bone mustard spoon, yellow with age, which I picked up for a nominal penny at the well-known Avon valley junk shop near the bridge over the river at Enford. Lately, however, I acquired a more up-to-date and much more efficient substitute which, even my friends agree, does the job better than either mustard spoon or marrow scoop. This useful aid may be yours too, for the taking.

Walking along a Wiltshire lane I came across a motor car indicator arm which had somehow parted company with its parent vehicle. I picked it up, removed the fractured orange indicator, and was left with a piece of chromium-plated metal not unlike a deeply grooved marrow scoop. I was at once struck by the resemblance and by the possibilities of my discovery.

I took the piece of metal home and later persuaded a friend to trim it up, smoothing the rough edges, for me to use in place of the old mustard spoon now in disuse.

This metal scoop is light to carry about in the fishing bag, easy to handle, effective to use and simple to keep clean. I showed it to my fishing classes in 1961 and have since seen many of those who attended them provide themselves with this simple and useful device.

I hope this idea won't tempt readers to help themselves to indicator arms from other people's motor cars. There is no need for desperate larceny of this kind for there are plenty to be had in scrap yards all over the country.

Securing the artificial nymph

When a nymph is tied on to the point of the cast but not in use, the practice of securing it by fastening the point of the hook in the cork handle of the rod risks blunting it and impairing its hooking power. In time too the cork handle becomes badly scarred and eaten away. Another disadvantage of this method of securing the nymph is that you must either use a cast several inches shorter than your rod or be prepared to put up with the inconvenience of having your cast loop reeled back through one or more of the rod rings. Your cast may also be weakened by the sharp angle at which it is bent at the terminal rod ring.

5. Weed-cutting Time: Discoloured Water and Floating Weed above Fisherton-de-la-Mere as the Author Fishes the Nymph.

6. THE WYLYE : THE AUTHOR FISHING ON A QUIET REACH ABOUT BRENTFORD MILL

A much better method of securing the nymph is to hold the rod by the cork handle in your right hand with the reel facing away from your chest; take the nymph in the fingers of your left hand and hook it on to one of the rings of the rod as far up it as your left arm can conveniently reach. Then run the fingers of your left hand back down the point of the cast from the nymph as far as is necessary to take the cast round the outside of the back of the reel beneath it, then forward and up towards the rod point. Holding the cast steady in this position, transfer the rod to your left hand and gently reel up until all is taut.

Weight and measure

Most fisheries impose a size limit based either on weight or length. Permanently in my fishing bag I carry an accurate spring balance and an old foot rule. Never try to weigh a live fish on a spring balance direct. Weigh it in your net and deduct the weight of the net.

A useful knife

I carry with me in my car at all times a remarkably useful knife which comes in handy for a variety of purposes. It is equipped with good cutting blades, a scissors, a probe, a marlin spike, a pair of tweezers, screw-drivers of two kinds, a tin-opener, a bottle opener, a corkscrew, various files, saws and other equally useful tools.

This knife was given to me by Lieutenant-General Hugh Pate Harris, who later commanded the United States Corps in Korea, when he and his aide, Captain Guy S. Meloy, fished the Wylye with me early in the 1961 season. We were the guests of Wing Commander and Mrs. Anthony Coke who were themselves away salmon fishing in Scotland at the time. My wife had set us up with an ample picnic basket and in honour of the occasion I took along a flagon of nicely mellowed dandelion wine and a flask of my choicest raspberry liqueur. During the morning we had a rough time in a testing wind but after luncheon we all fished as warriors should, with great panache and to good purpose.

★ 5 ★

Basic Technique

FISH the artificial nymph to a trout which you believe to be sizeable according to the rules of the water, and which you see feeding consistently below the surface. A nymphing trout is recognizable by the little movements it makes in the water as it lifts and turns to intercept nymphs and other small food creatures borne down by the current. These natural nymphs and other aquatic food particles may themselves be quite invisible, except in the most favourable conditions of light, background and visibility.

Nymphing trout look fairly lively in the water: wick, as we say in Lancashire. Their tails may be seen working, balancing the fish in the current, and they are said by fishermen to be "on the fin". From time to time, a feeding trout's jaws may be seen to open as it intercepts a natural nymph. Sometimes these jaws seem to whiten as the fish's mouth opens. At other times it may be inferred that something has been taken by the fish's apparent interceptory movement. Much can be learnt about nymphing trout by watching them as they feed in the water.

It always pays to weigh up a feeding fish before engaging it with an artificial. Some trout have decided leanings towards interception on the right or left side of their lies. Sometimes there are good reasons for such apparent preference. There was a trout at the tail of the middle run beneath Figheldean Bridge in 1960 which, I noticed, made all its interceptions to the right. Several times I ran a nymph down past its left flank without inducing any response then, the first time I cast with a little deliberate extra force to swing the nymph round above and to its right, it took the artificial voluntarily and readily. It was blind in the left eye and partly discoloured on the right flank.

For some years I have kept careful written records of all the fish I catch, and when I have time, I sometimes find it interesting to analyse certain details and statistics to throw light on straightforward questions which cannot always be answered simply. One such analysis concerned the trout I caught on nymph in the Upper Avon in the very dry summer of 1959.

Of the 35 trout I caught from the Avon on the nymph that season, no less than 30 were clearly seen in the water before an artificial was cast to them. When it is possible to see the fish, this is a much more reliable guide to its manner of feeding than speculation on rise forms alone. It is especially significant in rivers as naturally productive as the Upper Avon and Wylye. Concurrently with their function as sporting fisheries, these rivers are also nurseries for a tremendous stock of wild-bred trout. At any time during the season, it is probably true to say that not more than one feeding trout in twenty is of takable size. For this reason, rods are enjoined by the rules of their respective fisheries not to cast to rising trout until they have established that they are of warrantable proportions.

When it is not possible to see the trout in the water, either because of reflected light or in the dusk of evening, other means must be used to estimate their size. Helpful indications include the nature of the swirls made as the fish turn beneath the surface to intercept nymphs in the water, and past experience of the particular trout or usual run of trout which occupy a given lie as a rule.

This fascinating art loses something of its appeal when the take cannot be directly observed. This is one of the reasons why I do not trouble to fish the nymph as often as I might in the evening. Sometimes the nymph provides rewarding sport at this time, especially before sunset when the presence of much spent fly and possibly a late hatch of duns brings on the evening rise proper. Once the light begins to fail, detecting a take imposes the kind of strain I do not care to inflict on myself if I have merely gone down to the river for a bit of relaxation.

In open waters, reflected light may make it necessary to rely primarily on a study of rise forms to locate nymphing fish. The difficulty is that trout feeding well below the surface may not disclose their presence by a rise form at all. This I think explains why rods mainly accustomed to fishing this type of water regard the dry-fly as more rewarding than the nymph since the opportunities for using the nymph often go unnoticed. There are parts of the middle Test, at Leckford for example, where the broad river is open to the sky and reflected light makes it almost impossible in places to detect fish feeding below the surface. However if others are taking surface fly, the all-round fisherman should not feel discouraged. The dry-fly is after all the easier method and the one which I personally employ whenever the circumstances are propitious. I think too that in circumstances such as these, anglers not unnaturally find more pleasure in catching the trout on the dry-fly than on a nymph which they cannot see taken. It certainly explains why I catch more fish on the dry-fly than the nymph in the evening although I can usually detect a take in reflected light.

Of the trout I caught on nymph in 1959, 14 were seen lying over or at the tail of ranunculus beds, 13 were feeding over beds of water-celery, three were lying in deeper water among the ribbon weed and the remaining five were not directly seen at all before I cast to them. Two of these were lying close to the surface beneath the shelter of ranunculus fronds and disclosed their presence by repeated heavy swirls which enabled me to locate them and form a reasonable estimate of their size. Two were located by rise form alone and one was pointed out to me by the keeper.

Although trout feeding under water over weed beds are often said to be nymphing, a convenient term for subaqueous feeding, subsequent autopsies on such fish often disclose that they have in fact been taking a variety of food creatures in addition to nymphs themselves. I nearly always examine the stomach contents of the trout I take home, even of those which I subsequently give away to my friends. During the summer months these autopsies often provide a simple but convincing explanation of the futility of trying to catch nymphing trout on the dry-fly.

Modern nymph fishing is sometimes referred to by the expression "upstream nymph fishing". This may be misleading. The term serves to emphasize the fact that the nymph is not fished downstream in the old downstream wet-fly style, but in practice 23 of the trout I caught on nymph from the Avon in 1959 were taken on an artificial cast directly across the stream. I have tried to analyse the reasons for this.

In 1959, nearly all my day-time fishing was done before 1 p.m. (Summer Time) and on this river the light is most favourable on a sunny morning when fishing from the right bank (right when looking downstream, that is to say). It so happens that both banks of my two favourite wide shallows are thickly wooded to within a few feet of the water's edge. These are the broad shallows below the School of Infantry at Choulston and Alton shallows just below Figheldean Bridge. Wading is not allowed on the O.F.A water, therefore false casting to dry a fly is almost impossible when fishing to trout lying far across the stream. Nymphing fish which lie well out on the weed beds are consequently subjected to much less harrying with dry-flies, at least by right-handed fishermen, than is the case on more accessible reaches.

The screen of trees and bushes on the far bank of the river helps to combat reflected light and when trout can be seen feeding below the surface in places like these, the use of the nymph is not only logical but is probably the only way to present a fly capable of deceiving the fish.

DECEIVING THE TROUT

Deception is the basis of modern nymph fishing technique. *Aim to deceive your fish by offering it an imitation roughly resembling the natural nymph it is expecting to see at the level where it is expecting to see it and behaving as it is expecting it to behave.* But deception is only the first essential step in catching trout on the artificial nymph. You must not only deceive the fish, you must know when they have been deceived so that you can hook them effectively before they become aware of your cunning duplicity. Let us briefly review the practical means of achieving this.

Nymph pitching

The artificial nymph must be presented to the trout at the appropriate level in the water. It must therefore be so cast as to enable it to arc over and enter the water without alarming the trout or disturbing the surface and so impeding the vision of the nymph fisherman: an otter's entry.

Considerable practice is necessary to present the nymph at the appropriate level in the water, still correct for line. Careful judgment is necessary to balance such factors as the speed of the current, the depth at which the fish is feeding, and the known sinking capability of the artificial. Sometimes a nymph should be pitched into the water only a few inches upstream of a fish feeding close to the surface in slow-flowing water. At other times it may be necessary to pitch the nymph anything up to 15 yards above the fish's lie.

Lateral drag betrays the nymph fisherman, especially in fast-flowing water. Fish directly upstream to obviate the possibility of this whenever you can.

Effective striking

You must be keyed up to strike as soon as a trout takes your artificial between its jaws because the fish will eject the artificial the moment it discovers that it has been deceived. Trout seem capable of ridding themselves of a nymph quicker than they eject a dry-fly, possibly because it is smaller, more compact and less water resistant.

As the nymph is drifting down, palm the slack line in the usual way so that when you do use your rod tip, there is no delay in transmitting its strike to the business end of your tackle, the hook point. *Try to anticipate the moment for striking by picturing in your mind not only what is going on beneath the water, whether you can see it or not, but what you intend to cause to happen beneath the water.*

Any obvious movement by a trout close to the assumed position of your nymph may or may not be a take, but if you decide to wait and see, you are unlikely to find out more and if it was a take, you will have missed your chance to hook the fish.

Know this: in dry-fly fishing there are times when delay may be essential to ensure an effective strike; in nymph fishing, you cannot afford the luxury of any delay. The progress of the drifting nymph beneath the surface of the water is indicated by *the dipping point* of your cast. This is the place where the floating part of the cast turns down into the water as it is gradually drawn beneath the surface by the free-sinking artificial nymph. It is therefore not any one particular static point on the cast itself but more in the nature of a minute hole in the water through which you may expect to see the sinking cast accelerate slightly in the event of a fish taking your nymph, rather like the sally port of a belfry upper floor through which the bellrope descends sharply as the ringer on the floor below pulls on the bellrope sally.

When you are unable to see a fish take your artificial or to detect any action or movement on its part which might be construed as a take, you are obliged to rely mainly on the indication you notice at this dipping point to tell you when a take has in fact occurred. To observe, register and act on such an indication calls for sharpness on your part and above all, for informed anticipation, otherwise your strike will almost certainly be too late to be effective. This problem will be considered in greater detail later in this chapter.

A trout which has ejected a nymph after being once deceived may not readily accept another offer, at least not on the same day. Much depends on the standard of "education" of the fish you are trying for. Trout take anything from some minutes to a day or more to forget an experience of this kind. Pander to this understandable re-action by giving a missed fish time to regain its confidence. Do not try to deceive it with an artificial again until it has begun to feed once more and has fortified its self-confidence by successfully taking a number of natural nymphs.

Polaroid glasses

Polaroid glasses, readily obtainable nowadays, may be found helpful for looking into water on bright days. They combat glare and somewhat reduce the difficulties to which reflected light gives rise. They are valuable too for studying fish and other aquatic creatures in these conditions.

Polaroid glasses make it easier to detect when a trout takes your artificial nymph. The trouble is that if you rely largely on their aid right from the start, you are likely to miss them badly if for some reason you do not have them with you on a bright day. I found them quite helpful in the year when I first practised nymph fishing but I have not used them in recent years. Indeed, if I couldn't catch trout without wearing these things now, I should not consider myself competent to discuss practical nymph fishing.

NYMPH FISHING IN REFLECTED LIGHT

When reflected light effectively conceals a trout from view you must rely mainly on the floating part of your cast and other surface indications to tell you when your artificial nymph is taken. It is easier for you to anticipate these indications if you can visualise what is happening underwater as a feeding trout responds to your cast.

The take in nymph fishing may be either voluntary or induced. *A voluntary take* occurs when the fish seizes the nymph as it sinks after entering the water or at any time during the course of its free drift downstream. The significant point is that you remain absolutely passive, apart from methodically gathering in any slack line, until you detect the trout's voluntary acceptance of your artificial and strike on this signal.

An induced take occurs when the fish disregards the artificial nymph until you deliberately attract its attention to it by animating the nymph with a short sideways movement of the rod tip. This causes the artificial to swim or lift slightly in the water in a manner so realistic that the fish is impelled to take it, perhaps involuntarily.

There is usually a good chance of a voluntary take at the first offer when a trout is found feeding actively in streamy water over a bed of water-celery or ranunculus. Such a fish discloses its position in reflected light because its frequent movements, to capture agile natural nymphs or freshwater shrimps in transit between weed beds, give rise to bulging swirls on the surface. It is not unusual on a bright morning in the summer months to find several good trout so engaged in a comparatively limited area and with care and persuasion, the best of them should end up in your basket.

A small artificial nymph may attract the attention of a trout bulging in this manner although pitched as much as six feet upstream of its located position. Such fish not infrequently feed with great eagerness and the trout may shoot forward several feet to take the nymph. As it does so, the effect on the cast is a short but pronounced forward and downward tug which is most clearly to be seen at the dipping point.

The dipping point is the primary indicator of a take in nymph fishing in reflected light and in all circumstances in which you must rely on indications other than visual observation of the fish itself.

The tug on the cast indicated at this dipping point is due to the trout's own forward momentum and to its habitual tendency to level out in the water after taking food on or beneath the surface with its head slightly up-tilted. As the trout levels out its head descends with the nymph momentarily between its jaws creating a slight downward pull on the fine point of the cast which is nevertheless clearly registered at the dipping point.

When the artificial nymph alights close to and directly in front of a feeding trout, the fish may tilt up instantaneously but almost imperceptibly to take it. The only surface indication of such a take in reflected light will be the slight acceleration visible at the dipping point as the fish sinks down again when it levels out after taking. The indication itself may be trifling but if you are expecting it it is never-the-less significant. It is always easier to see what you expect to see, and to sharpen your reaction accordingly.

When the nymph pitches to the flank of a feeding trout, the fish will often turn aside violently to intercept it. The take in such a case is indicated by a sharp sideways tug on the cast as the fish turns back gripping the nymph in its jaws. In these cases there may often be a good preliminary indication of the intending take as the fish turns aside initially, creating a swirl visible on the surface. In thin water over water-celery or other weed, this may be followed by a distinct bow wave on the surface tracing the trout's course and ending abruptly as the fish goes about after taking the nymph. This creates a second swirl. To be effective, the strike must be made as the bow wave checks as by the time the second swirl shows on the surface, the trout will almost certainly have ejected the nymph, if it is a wild fish.

By assiduous attention to detail, I have worked out how to deceive trout into accepting my nymphs readily. Wherever I go to fish, I take it for granted that nymphing trout will accept my offer, even if it is little more than a bare o hook. They accept the nymph's appearance, controlled behaviour and, at times, even its taste, if it has taken several fish that day. But its consistency still defeats me. It is, after all, tempered steel! When a trout, a wild trout, takes an artificial nymph into its mouth it soon knows that it has been deceived and it ejects the artificial very quickly indeed, especially when the season is well advanced, by which time many of the surviving trout in a hard-flogged fishery have been deceived in this way several times and are becoming educated.

Even if the nymph falls slightly behind a trout, a feeding fish lying well up in the water will sometimes swing round and pursue the artificial downstream eagerly until it can overtake it and seize it from behind. This willingness to emerge from cover and hunt a nymph back has yielded me many seemingly inaccessible trout lying under the protection of low bridges, culverts and overhanging tree branches. Some examples from actual practice are given in Chapter Six.

Unfortunately, in reflected light there is hardly any indication at the dipping point when a fish takes an artificial nymph while swimming downstream on a fairly even keel, especially if it ejects the artificial before turning round to swim back to its lie. Only if the trout discloses its reaction by a preliminary swirl or its track by surface disturbance are you likely to be aware that the fish is chasing your nymph downstream.

On a number of occasions when I have been accompanying other fly-fishers under instruction but have perhaps been momentarily more favourably placed to see into the water, I have watched a trout follow a nymph yards downstream and then take as the angler concerned was on the point of recovering for another cast, not having realised that the fish was in pursuit. This explains how once in a while but, in my experience, rarely more than about once a season, trout are hooked "by accident" when one is nymph fishing.

It is sometimes possible to see into water adjacent to a position of a feeding trout concealed by reflected light. The induced take may be used on these occasions to persuade the trout to take the nymph in full view. I find this technique invaluable when I am demonstrating nymph fishing (see Chapter Six).

An induced take may also be used successfully after an anticipated voluntary take has failed to materialise. It is generally required when trout are feeding on some more obvious source of food such as minnows or sedge pupæ and when they are concentrating closely as they grub on the shallows for snail and caddis (generally called tailing) or are picking female olive spinners off their egg-laying sites underwater (browsing).

Trout feeding actively on minnows find these little fish such rewarding prey that they can rarely be bothered with nymphs, either natural or artificial. In July when great shoals of minnows concentrate on the gravelly shallows of the Upper Avon and Wylye to spawn, it is not unusual for powerful and voracious trout to emerge from their usual concealed lies in these rivers to take up remarkably exposed positions out on the thin water among the spawning minnows shoals. Most of the time the solid trout and tiny minnows appear to ignore one another completely but every now and again a trout will lunge savagely to take a nearby minnow. In reflected light such movements may create swirls and other surface disturbances which look extremely promising and it can be a frustrating, disappointing and very puzzling business trying to persuade the trout responsible for them to take a nymph.

I have had plenty of opportunities to study fish feeding in this way in the gravelly run at the right-hand edge of Choulston shallows below the School of Infantry at Nether-avon where conditions of excellent visibility usually obtain until about noon on bright summer days. Only on two occasions have I succeeded in catching trout on a nymph when they were actively minnowing in this way. Both times the artificial nymph passed so close to the trout that the slight movement employed in the induced take probably gave rise to an involuntary reaction on the part of the fish themselves.

Success with tailing trout is more readily achieved. The secret is to present the nymph to them at a moment when their concentration relaxes and their attention is no longer focussed on the bottom. This is all very well when the fish are clearly visible in the water but not quite so easy in reflected light unless the stream is so shallow that the fish's tail actually breaks the surface as it feeds. The moment of relaxed concentration is then indicated by the fish levelling out slightly and the disappearance of its tail below the surface. An account of nymph fishing for tailing trout is given in Chapter Eight.

When an induced take is considered necessary, the nymph should be pitched sufficiently far upstream, according to the strength of the current, to enable it to sink to the fish's level by the time it reaches a point immediately upstream of it. Movement is imparted with the rod tip at this point and if the timing is correct, both trout and grayling take the activated nymph almost involuntarily.

The amount of time you have in which to strike and hook the fish varies considerably according to whether the trout are educated wild fish or freshly stocked trout from a stew. I have known the latter take half the cast under water before they reacted to the deception. Some wild trout are pretty naïve too, in private and rarely fished waters, and I have known them take and eject a nymph several times in succession, vaguely puzzled but not unduly alarmed. Shy wild trout may realize their mistake very quickly indeed and eject the artificial immediately unless the point of the hook is made to take hold the instant their jaws close on the nymph. If you want to be sure of catching trout, credit them all with this speed of reaction until proved otherwise.

The technique of the induced take and the subsequent strike calls for much practice and the best time to obtain this is in the autumn when grayling are coming into peak condition. They take the nymph rather differently from trout and the surface indications, though pronounced, vary according to the size of the fish. Small grayling, especially, react to inducement very smartly and can eject the nymph with equal rapidity. Only their willingness to repeat the performance time and again enables the angler to speed up his reaction to the degree necessary to hook them successfully.

Dipping point indications can be made as clear cut as possible by constant attention to the state of the cast while fishing is in progress. Keep the point rubbed down with soft mud to enhance the nymph's free sinking capability. Grease the butt strand at intervals to keep it visible as well as to make it float. I find that four or five feet of thickly greased stout nylon is a great help in detecting a take in the turbulent water of a rough river as well as in reflected light on an open chalk-stream.

Many of the Wiltshire rivers, the Kennet, Wylye, Ebble and Nadder, flow in a general west-to-east direction. Sometimes if you are nymph fishing in the evening with the setting sun in your eyes, the ordinary problems of fishing in reflected light may be accompanied by real discomfort. I often find, however, that I can lessen this, either by crouching low, or by interposing a tree, bush, rick, barn, bank or other screen between my eyes and the sun. I have even taken advantage of a herd of inquisitive calves before now.

NYMPHS IN SLOW-FLOWING WATER

The duns which hatch from the slower reaches of rivers in summer include Slow-water Olives and Spurwings by day and Pale Evening duns at dusk on warm evenings. The nymphs of these species are among the fastest swimmers of all British Ephemeropterans. There are, broadly speaking, three ways in which trout take these nymphs in slow-flowing water: close to the surface, a moment before emergence; in mid-water; and near the bottom. Let us examine the circumstances in more detail.

Slow-water Olive duns may hatch well during the daytime throughout the summer months. They spend little time on their nymphal shucks at the time of their emergence. Indeed, on a dry, sunny day, they hatch so quickly from their carefully chosen launching sites on weed stems or stones not far beneath the surface that they appear to shoot straight up through it, like Polaris missiles fired from a submarine underwater. In favourable conditions of light this process may be seen happening time and again. It follows, therefore, that trout feeding near the surface during a hatch of these flies find it rather more profitable to take the nymphs when they are really vulnerable between launching and emergence than to try to capture the quick-escaping duns.

Cast precisely and deliver the nymph only slightly upstream of the feeding trout so that it will be presented to it accurately for line, a few inches beneath the surface. Little movement of the artificial should be necessary, apart from the essential slight upward lift imparted with the rod tip to simulate the natural nymph rising from its launching site to emerge on the surface as a dun.

The Pale Evening dun hatches best in late evening from the end of June until early September. Warm evenings in July are the commonest occasions for a hatch of this fly, but I saw it on a cold wet September evening in 1960 when Dr. Richard Jones and I were fishing the slow-flowing reach above Choulston hatches on the Upper Avon.

The duns are usually slow to leave their nymphal shucks, consequently trout find them easy prey. They take the duns freely on the surface when they hatch in numbers on warm evenings and there is nothing to be gained on these occasions by fishing the nymph close to the surface in the difficult conditions caused by failing light.

Trout feeding in mid-water may be stationary or cruisers: in either case they are usually remarkably alert for any movement which may betray the presence of any of the many food creatures on which they prey in that situation, including Slow-water Olive and Small Spurwing nymphs which have swum into mid-water from the bottom or the surrounding weeds.

The nymphs of both these species spend much of their time in and among the water weeds between which there is a good deal of active coming and going. Trout know this very well and they both intercept the nymphs in mid-water and actively chivvy them out of the weed itself.

To induce such a trout to take, present the nymph not more than a few feet away from it and at the depth at which you can see the fish feeding: the great charm of the art is its three dimensional scope. Attract the trout's attention to the artificial by imparting movement to it, if necessary; it shouldn't be if the nymph is sinking steadily like a natural nymph settling back into deeper water after a frolic from the weed or leaf debris on the bottom.

If the artificial sinks too far, and the trout seems likely not to notice it, impart slow, smooth lift to simulate a natural nymph rising into mid-water. Although the movement may appear slow, the artificial will in fact travel quite quickly enough through the water to simulate the characteristic movement of a natural nymph behaving in that way. In a quiet reach, a trout feeding in mid-water will sometimes unhurriedly follow the artificial some way downstream before eventually seizing it.

Finally, the trout may take Slow-water Olive and Spurwing nymphs in the deeper, sluggish reaches close to the bottom. Such a trout may be feeding several feet below the surface; its position and activity, though not disclosed by any surface movement, may nevertheless be seen in favourable conditions of light and background. There is a tree-enclosed pool on Major Robert Heywood-Lonsdale's water on the Wylye from which I have caught trout, grayling, roach and dace lying six feet below the surface but clearly visible from the bank.

In such cases, it is often necessary to cast the nymph 10 or 15 yards upstream to enable it to sink to the fish's level by the time it reaches it. Thereafter, the movement imparted to the artificial may be of two kinds: upward, to simulate a nymph rising into mid-water; or sideways and upwards, smartly, to suggest the characteristic rapid dart of a natural Slow-water Olive or Spurwing nymph.

The artificial should move at least a foot through the water, in either case, as a result of the action of the rod tip. If properly timed, this imparted movement will almost certainly be followed by an equally rapid reaction on the part of the trout, as it turns or lifts to take the nymph. You should accordingly be keyed up in anticipation of the fish's movement so that you can react quickly enough to strike as the fish closes its jaws over your artificial.

Grayling, I think, are smarter than trout when it comes to split-second last-minute rejection of an artificial fly or nymph. Very often I have seen a grayling, brought up to an angler's fly, recognize it the instant before taking as something of a suspicious nature and sheer off with great skill. The fish

7. The Avon Shallows Immediately Downstream of Figheldean Bridge.

8. Major Robert Heywood-Lonsdale Fishing his Water on the Middle Wylye at Bapton.

has perhaps done this several times in succession and has then been gratuitously described as "coming short". Grayling do focus oddly at times but they also have the ability to spot the flaws in dressing and presentation when they are so minded.

Each season begins on the Upper Avon with a biggish shoal of grayling in the midstream pocket just below the willow in the picture opposite page 80. This is only a few yards from the car parking site close to Figheldean Bridge and most people who begin or end their fishing at that popular site cannot resist having a throw at these grayling. During the course of a season a good many are caught and killed, for the rules of this fishery do not allow grayling to be returned. As the season wears on, the survivors become so adept at recognizing artificials that they must rank among the most sophisticated fish in Wessex. So highly do I rate their ability that I sometimes spend hours fishing for them, neglecting the trout just for the opportunity of pulling off a really satisfying piece of deception.

Having taken a nymph or fly, grayling are not as quick as trout to eject it, though they can sometimes be quick enough. But quick as trout are, I think roach are even quicker.

There was a time when roach and dace were quite plentiful in the Upper Avon, but since 1957, when they were severely netted, there have been very few. In that year my records show that I took 23, 21 of them on the artificial nymph; 6 in 1958, all on nymph; 4 in 1959, of which 2 took a nymph; 1 only, on nymph, in 1960; and 1 again in 1961, a dace of 14 oz. on nymph when fishing for grayling in a deep pool late in the year.

If I ever see a roach in one of the deeper pockets, I always like to have a go at it. Once hooked, roach put up an indifferent resistance but the charm lies in deceiving them. When a roach does take, it may not grip the artificial completely but tends to suck it in, open-mouthed, and then eject and suck several times more in rapid succession, as if cleaning the nymph. They want some hooking!

★ 6 ★

Some Problems and Their Solutions

A VIOLATION OF SANCTUARY

FIGURE 9 shows the favourite feeding lie of a pound trout caught in the inflow of a Wylye carrier stream above Fisherton de la Mere footbridge in the summer of 1960. The fish was quite well known to the rods who fished the water there regularly that season. It was regarded by most of us as something of a fixture because the surround-

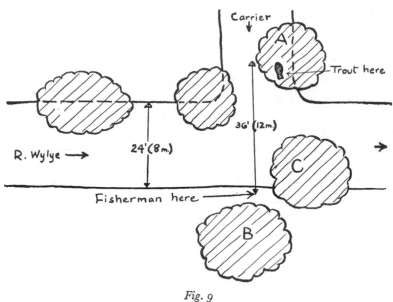

Fig. 9

A Wylye problem

82

ing trees were thought to have conferred on its lie the advantages, if not necessarily the privileges, of sanctuary.

The overhanging branches of Tree A made it impossible to put a dry-fly over or even near the fish. Moreover, the strong current in the main stream would quickly give rise to drag if an artificial were placed on the open water to the left of the trout's lie. This virtually precluded the use of the dry-fly to take this particular fish.

This did not prove a serious handicap, however, for on the day of its capture, the trout was seen to be nymphing and a fish feeding actively on nymphs can often be tempted out from under cover if its attention can be attracted to the artificial in some way. The problem in this case was how to present the nymph to the trout—how to pitch it into the water so that it would pass anywhere near the fish, in fact.

It was not possible to cast directly across the main stream because Tree B effectively blocked the back cast. This meant using a switch cast consisting of an upstream cast followed by a roll cast to change direction. Unfortunately the overhanging Tree C made it impossible to deliver the preliminary upstream cast from the bank immediately opposite the carrier inflow.

Figure 10 shows how the problem was solved in practice. This proved to be relatively easy, given a little luck among the willows on a rather windy day, and the hoped-for reaction on the part of the trout.

The preliminary upstream cast was made from Point 1 and the rod was then taken back a few yards downstream to Point 2. This was done smartly to keep the nymph near the surface on a tight line and so ensure a quick pick-up and smooth roll cast, delivered from Point 2.

This switch cast pitched the nymph into the carrier at Point 3. The moment it entered the water, it began to sink quickly, as an artificial must if it is to be effective in such cases. Then, before the current could cause it to drag unrealistically, lift was imparted with the rod tip, causing the nymph to swim lightly through the water.

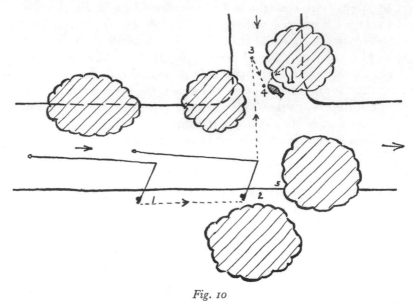

Fig. 10

Solution of the Wylye problem

This movement at once attracted the attention of the trout which swung across confidently to take the nymph at Point 4, opening its jaws to do so in a manner which left me in no doubt when to strike.

Living in fancied security, rarely if ever troubled by fly-fishers, this trout had grown fat and over-confident to the point of being easy to deceive. It was hooked, subdued after a lively fight, and finally netted out at Point 5.

PERSUASION IN SPRING

On a showery April day in 1961 I visited Mr. Charles Clore's water at Stype Grange on the Shal Bourne, a tributary of the Kennet. The little chattering bourne is quite narrow hereabouts, shallow in places and very clear. The water was stocked in 1960 and I wanted to see how the trout had fared. My first task was to catch one to establish its physical condition and to ascertain the nature of its stomach contents.

A gloomy day sometimes results in trout being easier to locate in water than is the case in bright sunshine. At any rate I spotted a good trout lying out in a shallow gravel run between some long thick clumps of emerald starwort a few yards downstream of a small low bridge on which I was standing. I thought this fish would suit my purpose very well so I went to my car, pulled on my waders, put up a rod and line, complete with ten-foot cast, mounted a tiny nymph on the point, entered the field flanking the stream, made a soft-footed detour and quietly got into the water well below the trout's lie.

But the fish must have seen me on the bridge, probably before I spotted it myself. It was no longer lying out on the gravel when I came within casting range of the place where I had first noticed it. I could not be sure what had happened to it but when I was within a few yards of the run in which it had been lying, the trout suddenly turned aside from beneath one of the starwort clumps where it had sought to hide and swam past me downstream, accelerating sharply as it did so. It looked to me to be a fish in surprisingly nice order for the time of year, but this was not enough for me to go on and somehow I had to find another fish and take it quickly, for I had much to do this day.

I was fortunate that the trout had elected to swim off downstream. If, as I would have expected, it had run upstream to the shelter of the bridge, it might have alarmed another good fish which I soon noticed in position there. I could just make out its tail close to the right abutment—that is the left abutment to me looking at the bridge from my position ten yards downstream.

The problem was how to present the nymph to the half-concealed trout protected as it was by the low bridge immediately above it. Three times I tried to shoot the nymph into the narrow tunnel-like space over and beside the fish, but on each occasion the wind blowing through it checked the fine point of the cast, causing the nymph to check too and then drop back into the water behind but well clear of the fish's tail. This tail, just visible to me, was moving freely enough to suggest that the trout was on the watch for food drifting down in the current and I toyed with the idea of trying to tackle it from above, a move which often succeeds with the dry-fly against shy fish. But there was no reason to suppose this fish was shy, especially so early in the year, and I decided instead not to be quite so ambitious with my casting. I bit a foot off my point and pocketed the spare length: never, ever, throw bits of nylon either into the water or on to the banks—it causes immense suffering to birds and wildfowl which tangle in it. I then re-tied my nymph on and prepared to make the fish do the hard work for me.

I dropped the little nymph into the partly sheltered bay opening immediately downstream of the abutment edge and just to the left of the fish's tail. As the artificial sank in the shallow water of the quiet bay, I imparted slight lateral movement, causing the trout to turn at once, presumably sensing the presence of the nymph behind it, and pursue it. I saw the fish's jaws open and close quite distinctly as it took the nymph viciously. This trout, too, did the opposite of what I expected. Instead of seeking the cover of the bridge it ran straight out into the open water in front of me and jumped rapidly four times in succession.

No fish can keep this sort of performance up for long and this one duly came to the net. It was a lovely trout, silvery in colour and already in excellent condition, as it should have been, for its stomach contents included a variety of valuable and nourishing protein-content invertebrates.

INDUCEMENT IN SUMMER

One hot sunny afternoon in the summer of 1960 I was fishing the Wylye above Boreham Mill with Sergeant Cruse of the Warminster police. I used a nymph to take out an old lean fish, going back badly, which we knocked over the head as an act of mercy. I then caught a brace of nicely conditioned pounders on the dry Olive. With these fish I was content but my companion had been interested in the induced take technique which I had employed to get rid of the thin fish and he asked me to show him it again in practice.

It took a little time to find another trout feeding under water, and when I at last thought I had located one, reflected light prevented me from pointing out its position clearly and threatened to obscure the proceedings during the demonstration. However, I explained where the fish was lying, well down in three feet of water, and added that I would float the nymph down the deep run a foot or two to the fish's left where the visibility was better and the bottom was clearly observable. I said I would try to induce the trout to move across into this run and take in full view.

By casting well upstream I was able to give the nymph time to sink to the required level, and just before reaching the trout's area, I lifted it with my rod tip, keeping the slack line well gathered in my left hand. Immediately the trout swung across into clear view and took the nymph. Not wanting to hook it, I did not strike and we had an equally good view of its sharp ejection of the artificial and the rather bemused head shaking and jaw snapping which sometimes follows this discovery of deception.

Today Sergeant Cruse is himself a master of this technique which I have seen him employ to good effect both on the Avon and Wylye and on the Duke of Somerset's lake at Maiden Bradley.

BACKLASH TECHNIQUE

The shepherd's crook type of cast often mentioned in connection with dry-fly fishing practice is a most useful aid in nymph fishing, when it comes off. I think it is impossible to be sure of throwing a forward cast curving round to the right, to a right-handed caster, but with practice and some luck it is sometimes possible to cast forward and curve the point round to the left, especially if your cast is made up on the lines suggested in Chapter Four, and the wind is not awkward.

Depending on the degree of force employed, the leftward curl can be anything from a slight deflection to quite a sharp turn. To bring it about, hold your rod parallel with the water, or as near parallel as the bank herbage allows, do not have too much shooting line drawn off the reel, and deliver your cast with rather more violence than is necessary to take out the slack line. Aim at a point well above the water. The nymph will be propelled forward and, as the slack is taken up fully, will recoil in greater or less degree according to its own momentum at the time. This recoil or backlash, with practice, is used to swing the nymph round to the left of its original trajectory.

We have a carrier on the Wylye which rejoins the main

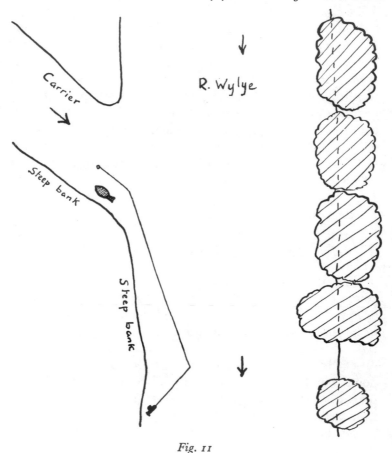

Fig. 11

The carrier inflow on the Wylye at Bapton

river at a point where it flows between high banks caused by wartime dredging to convert that charming stream into an anti-tank ditch. The carrier itself comes in between its own high banks. There is often a good trout in a lie in the carrier mouth, just around the corner, as it were, from the main river. A dry-fly rarely succeeds in this position. Apart from the fact that it is impossible to see when it is taken, the fish lying in that run are nearly always taking food beneath the surface. I know. I have caught and examined many of them.

I should mention that the opposite bank is thickly wooded otherwise it would not be difficult to cover a fish in the carrier mouth from that side. Fig. 11 shows the carrier mouth diagrammatically and the manner in which the backlash cast can be used to present a nymph to a fish in position in the popular lie.

Although the dipping point itself is usually invisible round the corner of the high bank, the floating part of the cast usually gives a clear indication of a take by suddenly checking or even moving upstream slightly as it is drifting down after the cast has been made.

★ 7 ★

Weed-Cutting Time

THE EFFECTS OF WEED-CUTTING

CHALK-STREAMS support a particularly lush growth of water weed, notably water buttercup or ranunculus, as it is more generally called, water-celery, star-wort and a variety of so-called pondweeds (*Potamogeton* spp.). By the time the main Mayfly hatch is over in early June (some rivers are somewhat later than this), the rapid growth of spring and early summer threatens to obstruct much of the watercourse on some fisheries. This not only interferes with fishing itself, making it difficult both to put a fly over a trout and to handle it effectively if it is hooked, but may cause the water level to rise sufficiently to soften and even flood the banks. To prevent this happening, and to tidy up the river generally, most chalk-stream fisheries undertake a major programme of systematic weed-cutting at this time.

Weed is trimmed at various times during the course of the year, according to the circumstances and the labour force available, but the main weed-cutting usually takes place in June and early July, both in the river itself and along the banks. In Wiltshire we have a convention which we try to observe that weed-cutting should not begin until June 15th, should be completed by mid-July, and should, if possible, not be carried out at week-ends, when many rods find their only opportunities of sport.

Weed-cutting badly discolours the water immediately downstream of the scene of operations and gives rise to un-attractive and often unpleasant fishing conditions. Great rafts of shorn ranunculus tresses and other cut weed and

90

bankside herbage follow one another downstream in con-
tinous succession for hours on end, interfering considerably
with fishermen seeking sport with a fly rod. Many anglers
so dislike fishing when weed is coming down that they stay
away from the river altogether at this time. By so doing,
they undoubtedly deprive themselves of numerous opportunities of catching feeding fish with the artificial nymph.

Understandably, much of the cut weed is swarming with
such trout food creatures as freshwater shrimps, caddis
grubs, various species of water snails, water lice, and, of
course, the nymphs and larvae of upwinged flies. Feeling
themselves cut adrift from the fancied security of their
former habitat, many of these creatures quit the floating
weed masses to look for more stable shelter in the river
before they are carried too far downstream.

Both trout and grayling soon become aware of these sub-
aqueous happenings, finding rich protein pickings drifting
to them in the currents in which they lie in hopeful expectation. Fish soon feel encouraged to feed readily under water
on a variety of these food creatures, perhaps somewhat
emboldened by the extra cover afforded by discoloured
water. In so doing, they lay themselves open to deception
by the nymph fisherman.

At the same time the quality of the dry-fly fishing falls
off each year on some chalk-streams after the Mayfly hatch
is over; another reason why fewer people bother to fish these
rivers during the daytime at this period. Some people seem
to imagine that the trout are suffering from a kind of hang-
over at this time, attributable to a surfeit of Mayflies, which
causes them to stop feeding altogether! What has given rise
to this widespread but fallacious belief? To find the answer,
we must first look back at the happenings of the weeks prior
to the Mayfly hatch.

The appearance of fly steadily builds up to a climax
during May. Heavy falls of Hawthorn-fly may be expected
during the first ten days of the month, especially after a mild
winter and early spring. Sometimes, too, there are Spring
Black Gnats on the water as well. Upwinged duns come up

in increasing numbers as the days lengthen and insectivorous birds flock to the valleys, both from the close surrounding downs and from as far afield as the distant Drakensburg Range. Among these duns are several species of Olives, Iron Blues which sometimes hatch well in showery windy conditions, Small Spurwings, Slow-water Olives, and a sprinkling of Turkey Browns and Yellow May duns, both species readily recognizable but of less significance than the others to the fly-fisher and his quarry.

All this fly is calculated to produce some of the best dry-fly fishing of the trout season, at least until September. But not all trout are attracted to the surface by small fly, however diverse and numerous. Rich feeding is available under water throughout the chalk-stream season and not unnaturally this is where many trout, particularly the larger fish, obtain the bulk of their food. But during the Mayfly period they grow used to seeing numbers of fat Greendrakes and large spent Mayfly Spinners and they then turn to this satisfying diet, seeking it where it is available in the greatest quantity for the least effort—on the surface.

Do not overlook the tremendous increase in sub-aqueous food supplies at this time. Freshwater shrimps are multiplying freely; they may produce as many as seven broods in the course of a year. The river teems with young snails, clinging to weed stems and stones on the bed, and occasionally drifting with the current, close to the surface, on local migrations (see page 103). Minnows concentrate in big vulnerable shoals preparatory to spawning. Trout fry may themselves be plentiful, scattered about in their separate territories in the little bays and inlets: all trout from yearlings upwards are merciless cannibals by nature. Most important of all, the big summer generation of nymphs of many prolific species of upwinged flies is developing in the water.

When the Mayfly season ends, therefore, it is scarcely surprising that trout cease to find surface feeding worthwhile, especially as when Mayfly hatches fall off, so too do daytime hatches of small fly of many species whose main emergence periods occur in spring and autumn.

The inevitable result is that trout rise less freely. There isn't much for them to rise to, at least not until the evening when some duns prefer to hatch as the temperature drops and when a fair amount of spent fly may also help to bring fish up to feed on the surface.

There is one important exception: the Pale Watery dun often hatches in sufficient numbers on June days to keep enough trout interested to make fishing worthwhile. Sport is quiet and often rather slow after the excitements of the Mayfly period and the chances of finding large fish rising are undoubtedly less. Many times, too, I have seen trout completely ignore fast-hatching Pale Wateries on a sunny June day. Even so, they can still be caught, but how?

SOME JUNE BASKETS ANALYSED

To find out how I catch June trout in practice, I carefully analysed my daytime baskets from the Upper Avon for the three consecutive seasons 1958–1960 inclusive. I confined the analysis to this river because it is reputed to be a difficult one after the Mayfly, though not, perhaps, the most difficult.

The Upper Avon Mayfly hatch begins nowadays about May 16th, reaches its peak by the 25th and tails off by the first week of June when, on this river, the main weed-cutting operations start. I picked on 1958–1960 because these three years represent a fairly wide range of weather and water conditions.

The following table records only trout caught between 9 a.m. and 5 p.m. and not those taken in the evening when hatches of duns and the presence of much spent fly on the water make them relatively easy to catch:

Date	Trout caught	Artificial responsible
7 June 1958	2	Nymph, 2
12 June 1958	6	Nymph, 6
17 June 1958	2	Nymph, 2
28 June 1958	6	Nymph, 6

Date	Trout caught	Artificial responsible
6 June 1959	2	Nymph, 2
13 June 1959	3	Nymph, 3
20 June 1959	3	Nymph, 3
27 June 1959	4	Nymph, 3; dry-fly, 1
4 June 1960	4	Nymph, 3; dry-fly, 1
11 June 1960	4	Nymph, 4
18 June 1960	2	Nymph, 2
25 June 1960	6	Nymph, 6
Totals:	44	42, Nymph
		1, Red Spinner
		1, Pale Watery Dun

From this table it can be seen that on two occasions in 1958 and one in 1960, the limit of three brace of trout was caught before 5 p.m. As a matter of interest it was subsequently reached after 5 p.m. on five of the other dates listed in the table. Now eight limit baskets on twelve fishing days hardly reflects a picture of hopeless prospects. Even during the daytime, the average catch in June was about two brace. The most significant feature of these daytime figures is, of course, the proportion of trout caught on the artificial nymph: 42 out of a total of 44.

My diaries record that the trout taken during the daytime in June were almost all gorged with food of various kinds: nymphs, caddis, snails large and small, shrimps, crayfish, minnows and trout; but, apart from an occasional spent spinner or Pale Watery dun, little in the way of hatched fly.

The Mayfly, far from satiating trout, stimulates their appetites, to satisfy which they feed voraciously beneath the surface. I see them at it every year, at weed-cutting time. And if you would catch them, you must fish for them below the surface too.

SOME LOCAL ADJUSTMENTS

Weed-cutting methods vary, and some people have strong views on how it should be carried out. Usually, when a chain scythe is used, cutting is done by working upstream. With a hand scythe it is often done downstream. This is the method I prefer. Trout are surprisingly bold at this time, and after cutting has been in progress for a few days, some may be found feeding within a yard or two of the scythe, taking the nymphs and other creatures in the water. Weed bars trimmed off on a reach one day are likely to have feeding fish lined up behind them the next. After they have had a day or two to settle down to the new conditions, and have enjoyed the plentiful food supply which accrues to them at this time, they feed confidently and can offer good sport to the observant nymph fisherman.

Where the weed is cut close to the bottom, it might seem to deprive trout of much of their shelter. Most of the fish will find cover in the weed bars, of course, but it is astonishing how little is required to hide even quite large trout.

At no time is this more apparent than when we are using electric fishing apparatus to collect up large trout from the small carriers and sidestreams in which they have spawned. We do this each year in March and April, returning the adult fish to the main river so that their progeny may enjoy the benefit of nursery conditions free from the cannibalistic attentions of their parents. The electrode, attached to a big landing net on a pole handle, draws the trout out from its shelter as if by magnetism and the fish is then netted and promptly transferred to a tank in the punt in which the engine is mounted. Almost negligible cover sometimes gives up not one trout but several, while an old root mass may produce a dozen or more.

In April 1961 we had almost reached the top of one of our main nursery streams, the Nine-mile River, when we came to a place where an old willow branch had fallen into the narrow watercourse, here not more than six feet wide. This timberfall had trapped a mass of smaller branches, twigs, old leaves and other litter. From beneath it all we extracted scores of trout, some between two and three pounds in weight, with the spectators forming stickles up- and downstream of the site to prevent any fish escaping.

It is a rough old place, the valley of the Nine-mile River. Much of it is marshy, with clumps of blackthorn here and there, blooming like snow in the early spring and bearing a crop of sloes in October, many of which end up in my cottage for the purpose for which God doubtless intended them. Some yards back from the low-lying, rush-grown watercourse is a tangle of ivy-clad hawthorns beneath which is a profusion of nettles. There you may hear the nightingale sing, not only at night as you walk from Sheep Bridge to Bulford village, but in the noonday sun and through the sweet showers of late April. And there, among the blackthorn copses, the longtailed tits create their exquisite feather-lined, lichen-camouflaged nests and the young water-mint beneath your feet is crushed and reaches your nostrils like a scent from long ago.

TACTICS

After the mid-summer weed-cutting is over, it is usual to find a number of weed rafts lodging here and there along the edges of the river, the thick tresses perhaps being trapped initially by dense herbage growing out from the bank, or by low-slung tree branches, projecting roots, old timber piles, camp sheathing and such-like obstructions.

Cut weed may also lodge on shallow places in midstream and around the upstream ends of bridge piers and hatchways. Even if all these weed lodgements are moved on as they occur at the time of the cut, some of them seem to be regularly replaced and reinforced by weed arriving in the fishery after floating down from other reaches farther upstream.

Many invertebrate food creatures acceptable to trout which have not succeeded in quitting these weed masses before they settled on these sites continue to live in them and may, indeed, be joined by others from the waters nearby. An examination of samples taken from these weed rafts discloses quite a complex ecological structure.

Here and there some of these weed rafts are understandably popular with trout both as food larders and as shelter, affording alternate covered lies to the more exposed runs where the streamy currents emerge from freshly trimmed weed bars.

Because such trout may not be seen does not necessarily mean that they are not there, taking full advantage of the excellent facilities which the weed rafts afford. Indeed, my experience with certain weed rafts which regularly form against permanent snags in the rivers I fish, are that they may continue to yield trout as long as they remain in position, perhaps for the entire duration of the trout-fishing season.

Several fish may occupy feeding positions in line ahead, concealed from view beneath the edge of a long raft of cut weed extending, perhaps, ten or more yards downstream. When you locate such a raft, you have to make a mental appreciation of whether this is likely or not, and to deduce just where the fish are likely to be lying from your knowledge of the water and the trout it holds and, perhaps, in the light of what you may already know about the raft and its usual tenants.

The chances are that the best, certainly the strongest, trout will be lying in the position farthest upstream. You then have to decide whether to pitch your nymph with a view to catching this good fish, forfeiting others in downstream positions which will almost certainly be scared or made cautious in the process, or you can have a shot at taking each in turn beginning at the downstream end of the weed raft. If necessary the smaller fish, which although takable may not be creditable, may be released, preferably without handling. I believe it is reasonable for a fly-fisher in pursuit of a worthy trout to hook, gently free and transfer lesser trout which might otherwise give the game away. I do not, myself, go fishing for trout, catching and releasing them one after the other. Whether I kill my trout to take home or turn them loose, I generally stop fishing when I have caught the number prescribed in the rules of the water as the limit. Sometimes, of course, one fishes in accordance with the express wishes of one's host: he may want old fish killed, up to a set number, but all growing fish, however large, put back. Then you try to pick out the old fish. Normally, to fish on after catching the limit only serves to educate fish, most of which are already difficult enough and in some cases, at least, is almost bound to result in injury and, perhaps, unnecessary suffering.

If conditions of light and visibility are favourable it may be possible to see fish clearly as they move out to intercept a nymph which has been cast so as to drift close past the edge of a weed raft. When fish cannot be seen because of reflected light you must keep a careful eye on your dipping point for the indication of a take. If you have run your nymph down beneath the edge of a weed raft two or three times without response, try again, first imparting lift near the upstream end of the weed raft, then again with animating lift about half-way along, finally trying lift at the tail end. Mostly the best fish are to be found at the upstream end.

Weed rafts of reasonable size, which do not obstruct the watercourse and constitute useful shelter for fish and food creatures, perform a useful function in a fishery, but large weed masses of this kind are undesirable. They interfere with the flow, trapping silt and other harmful deposits, they quickly become fouled to a quite disgusting extent by voles, moorhens and wildfowl, attracting masses of small black flies, and in time they decay, taking tremendous toll of the oxygen content of the water as they do so. Despite the labour entailed, I like to rid the fishery I look after of unpleasant, indeed noxious, eye-sores of this nature as soon as possible.

The presence of weed in the river inevitably results in a good deal of silt being trapped anyway. In this silt live many creatures, among them lampreys which have been called sand-prides in Wiltshire since time out of mind. On several occasions when my daughter has been helping me in the river at weed-cutting time, she has had lampreys wriggle into her shoes. Lampreys are most in evidence during the electric fishing of sidestreams. Where these flow between silt banks the current from the electrode pushes great

numbers of lampreys out of the silt so that they may easily
be picked up by hand.

Sometimes a dabchick is smartened up by the electric
machine. Under water, dabchicks are scarecrow creatures
anyway, looking rather like newly feathered chickens, but
when livened up by a bit of electricity, they must surely
present the most undignified sight in all the chalk country.

A dabchick has a mighty quick eye, however, and when
he surfaces without knowing you are there, will spot you at
once, twenty yards away, and duck under with a splash.
Compare this with the water vole. This lovable, damp,
hairy, blunt-nosed, dark-eyed animal will let you approach
within a yard, if you are cautious, before he sees you. The
difference is, of course, that the vole is vegetarian whereas
the dabchick has the quick eye of a hunter. In this respect
he resembles that other pirate of the chalk valleys, the heron.

One of the snags about fishing at weed-cutting time is the
discoloration of the water. Discoloured water is a disadvantage in nymph fishing, whatever you may think about
its effect on sport with the dry-fly. It is difficult to be sure
why this should be so. Trout seem capable of detecting and
taking insects, both natural and artificial, floating on the
surface in quite thick water, possibly because they show up
in silhouette against the sky. Nymphs seem more apt to go
unnoticed. The best chance of rectifying this is by the
application of a little movement to the artificial, imparted
with the rod tip.

The efficacy of this method is fairly easy to demonstrate,
provided that you can locate a feeding trout in somewhat
discoloured water. A delicately presented nymph may be
allowed to drift past the trout unheeded by the fish unless
it passes very close indeed to its head. This may happen
two or three times running. If you then cast a little farther
upstream so that your nymph sinks just below the fish's level
by the time it reaches a point about a foot upstream of it
and you then impart lift to the artificial in front of the fish,
the trout will nearly always take it smartly, almost as if you
have triggered off an inevitable reaction. But you must move

the nymph in a life-like manner. If you cause it to drag, you get the same reaction as you do to a dragging dry-fly.

When I am wading on the well-aerated shallows at weed-cutting time, I see many female spinners alight on my waders just above water level and crawl down them in search of egg-laying sites below the surface. The spinners most in evidence in June are those of the Olive, the Small Olive and, sometimes, a few late Iron Blues. It is noticeable, too, that if I shake them free a foot under water, they at once bob up to the surface again. Spent female spinners drifting down with the current are also very close to the surface. They float in, if not exactly on, the surface film. At times this film seems more elastic than others.

Fish taking spent spinners will also usually take an artificial nymph fished just awash. Trout often lie just downstream of the piers or abutments of bridges where they intercept spinners which have just laid their eggs beneath the water along the masonry, brickwork and concrete of these structures. At weed-cutting time they get the best of both worlds, for besides the spent fly, they intercept nymphs emerging from weed masses caught up in hairpin formation around the upstream points of bridge piers. Don't take my word for it, catch them and examine their stomach contents.

You learn much about fish and fly when you tend a fishery and cut weed by hand. The temperature of the water varies considerably in mid-summer, especially on a hot day, according to the depth, the strength of the current and the degree of shade afforded. All upwinged flies have an optimum temperature above which their nymphs inevitably die. Considerable local underwater migration of nymphs is therefore to be expected.

The species of fly found in a stream depends much less on mean conditions than on the existence of favourable microhabitats suitable for the individual species concerned. Some species seem unable to tolerate temperatures exceeding 20 degrees Centigrade. Others can survive temperatures approaching 30 degrees.

Spurwings like relatively warm water although they may

be seen hatching from various different types of reach on a river and, of course, even from still water. Remember, however, that quite fast cool chalk-stream shallows sometimes end in a check bend composed partly of sun-warmed backwater where Spurwing nymphs, and perhaps nymphs of the Slow-water Olive may be found. The criterion is not the superficial external character of the reach from which the duns appear to emerge but the existence in it of a viable microhabitat suited to the particular species concerned, in its larval and nymphal stages.

When fly production is under consideration, it is sometimes forgotten that it is with these latter stages of the insect that the river keeper is concerned. The winged stages are merely the proof of the pudding. Much of the work I do on a chalk-stream fishery is aimed at producing hatches of fly by providing conditions suitable for the development of the larval and nymphal forms of the main sporting species. It is quite pointless in a sporting fishery to have stocks of good trout if you have no fly to induce them to move in such a way as to offer sport, either to nymph or dry-fly.

DRIFTING SNAIL

Gunville at the top of the Syrencote reach of the Avon is an attractive place at any time. When the season begins there is a delicate grey-green tint of spring on the budding willows, deepening rapidly to jade as the leaf opens, cheered on by half the chiffchaffs in the chalk country and the ecstatic trilling of many willow warblers. Then, at Mayfly time, the lush meadows flanking the hatch-pool are knee-deep in buttercups and hawthorn blossom scents the mild air. These May flowers blush as the green and gold of their month gives way to the heady elderflower, whitening the copses in early June. Later in the month, the wild rose riots on every hedgerow and the cuckoo's hoarse complaint tells me that summer's tide is full.

One evening late in June 1959 when weed-cutting was still in progress I went to fish the quiet canal-like impounded reach of the Avon above Gunville hatch-pool. The air was warm and still and great swarms of male spinners of several species were dancing about the water-meadows. In similar conditions some days earlier, I had killed three good trout on the pheasant tail Red Spinner and when I had put my tackle together I confidently tied on one of these artificials and walked across to the bank path to wait for the evening rise to begin.

I passed the time of day with George Marks who lives in the pretty thatched cottage beside the hatch-pool: a tall, slim, upright man, burnt dark by the sun and the wind, handsomely so, with the gentle courtesy you still find, here and there, in these parts; he would, I think, have delighted Velazquez in his prime.

I found, on this particular evening, that a tremendous quantity of cut weed had floated down from the reaches above. The hatchway had become completely choked, as is not unusual at weed-cutting time, and the thick ranunculus tresses had built up above them in a solid mass extending almost 50 yards upstream, considerably reducing the flow of the river and raising the water level so that parts of the path along the bank were already awash.

Just before sunset several fish began to rise quietly in the almost still water above the scum-fringed weed blockage. The evening hatch of duns had not yet started and it therefore seemed unlikely that fish were taking nymphs so close to the surface. The rise forms, of a gentle sipping nature, were more suggestive of trout taking spent fly. I couldn't see any spinners in the surface film but that did not necessarily mean that there were none coming down.

There were three fish moving steadily within casting distance and I covered each in turn with the Red Spinner, all quite delicate and satisfactory offers, not difficult to achieve on such a calm, still evening. All three ignored my fly completely but continued to rise steadily, sometimes shifting position slightly as they did so.

I realised that for once the pheasant tail Red Spinner was not going to work for me in the evening. There are only a few occasions each season when this happens and by careful observation I can generally deduce which particular fad has given rise to the fish's single-minded selectivity and take appropriate action to present them with an imitation of the fly claiming their undivided attention. But on this June evening I failed to notice anything which would help me to choose a logical substitute.

I recalled that during the previous week we had experienced unusually heavy flush hatches of Broadwings, one of the minute *Caenis* species which I had not encountered in quantity on this river before. They are really a bit too small to imitate satisfactorily but thinking that perhaps spent spinners of this tiny species might be coming down, I picked out the smallest fly in my box, an old and battered Tup's Indispensable nymph dressed on a ooo hook, which I had bought from a shop some years earlier before I knew anything much about nymph fishing. It had lost all its original fresh colours and almost all its modest hackle so that all that remained on the tiny hook was a bit of bluish grey woolly thorax, dull and dark with age and long, if unprofitable service. It was the kind of nymph which has to be licked and sucked and spat on and swore at before it will sink, yet now, in its old age, its hour had almost come.

When I cast this weary artificial to one of the fish rising persistently in mid-stream it was promptly taken by what proved to be a solidly built 12-inch trout. As I took the fish from my landing net, conscious of the soundness of my reasoning, it disgorged a quantity of small bluish-black snails which made me think again. Looking into the trout's mouth, I saw a great many more in its gullet.

Since the river was cleaned in 1953, these snails have become very numerous in the Upper Avon and during the summer months it is not unusual to find that they constitute a high proportion of the stomach contents of both trout and grayling. Indeed, in shallow water both species can often be seen grubbing for them along the bed of the river.

I have kept snails of this type under observation at my home from time to time and I know that on warm evenings they sometimes float to the top of the water, shell down and fleshy part uppermost, to drift gently but by no means helplessly up against but just beneath the surface film, as nymphs sometimes do when they have a struggle to hatch. The snails possess some slight propulsive power in completely still water but in the river they can, of course, take advantage of the currents to enable them to migrate locally downstream and possibly in this way to seek a fresh microhabitat more to their liking when they so desire. They have the ability to sink to the bottom at will, rather like a submarine dives after blowing its tanks.

The capture of this first trout suggested that one of these evening snail migrations was then in progress in the river. It was my good fortune, after making a quite reasonable but, as it proved, wholly false assumption to have chanced on an acceptable imitation in my fly box. Before the light failed I profited from this fortuitous discovery to the extent of a further brace of good trout, both crammed with snail, a game old cock grayling, and a large dace: a fairly varied basket by chalk-stream standards, especially from so unusual an evening rise.

★ 8 ★

A Memorable June Day on the Upper Test

O N 6th June, 1961, I fished the uppermost beat of
the River Test, the Polhampton Mill reach of the
Laverstoke Estate water, at the kind invitation of
Mr. J. C. Marsden. It was a lovely day, probably the hottest
of the year up to that time. I left home soon after nine
o'clock and found Bere Mill beyond Overton without any
difficulty, thanks to the clear directions I had been given
over the telephone by Mr. Charles Smith, who has charge
of this remarkable water. He and Mrs. Smith came out to
welcome me and took me in for a cup of coffee before we
set off. The swallows nesting in the porch knew I was a
stranger and protested.

Mr. Smith told me that the top beat at Polhampton was
available if I cared to try it, as he hoped I would, alternatively I could fish in Laverstoke Park where he thought
the fish might be more accommodating. I elected to have
a go for the more sophisticated quarry about which I had
read and heard a good deal. I didn't much mind the fish
beating me but I was very interested to find out just how
they would do it. I was soon to learn.

We set off with Charles Smith leading me first through
Laverstoke Park, pointing out the beat where I might like
to fish if I wanted a change from Polhampton. On arrival
at the mill he helped me to carry my gear from the car to
the fishing hut where he pointed out the main features of
the beat. The river isn't wide here, perhaps about eight to
ten yards, and very shallow, scarcely knee-deep anywhere,
and quite incredibly clear even by chalk-stream standards,

with a lot of weed. The most deceptive thing about this pellucid water is that the trout do not look anything like as big as they really are, a curious feature.

It was about noon and too hot for any significant hatch of fly. Indeed, apart from an occasional Iron Blue and a few Blue-winged Olives, I saw no duns all day. The only surface disturbance was caused by an odd trout tailing in the weed beds. However, some of the large fish which were obviously plentiful on this beat were moving underwater. They were lying for the most part in the gravelly runs between weed beds, ideally positioned to intercept drifting nymphs, freshwater shrimps and the like. The presentation of an artificial to these fish was by no means easy. It had to be placed in quite a narrow channel between the weeds and with a dry-fly, drag occurred almost immediately. Also the shadow of the cast, even of the fine point, was quickly apparent to the fish and I perceived the reason why Charles Smith had offered me some beautifully tapered casts of extreme fineness which I had declined with thanks.

Now the trout here are all wild fish and extremely shy. This is hardly surprising because the exceptional clarity of the water makes them keenly alive to any movement within view. It was therefore necessary to throw a very long line and the day was by no means windless so this too required some care. Indeed, in these circumstances, my best was sometimes just not good enough for this beat is indeed a connoisseur's water, if ever I saw one.

When all was ready to begin, Charles Smith drew my attention to one or two fish lying near a little weir just upstream of the fishing hut. There was a large black trout moving just downstream of the weir, feeding with uptilted tail much of the time, grubbing for food among the water-celery on the bed of the stream. I couldn't interest this fish in my nymph at all after failing to bring it up to an Iron Blue. I have since wondered whether perhaps its sight was failing. Discoloration and partial loss of sight frequently go together in trout.

In the open gravelly pocket just above the weir, this

perhaps is an ambitious description for a six-inch fall of water, a nicely shaped pale fish was lying. I wasn't certain that it was a takable size and I was shaken when my companion estimated its weight at well over 2 lb. I laid my cast nicely on the water, drifting the nymph down a foot to the trout's left. It moved over to inspect my artificial carefully. It is questionable whether the trout would have taken it if I hadn't removed it. Next throw, the trout just turned to look but did not swing across to take. The third throw it ignored completely. This was clearly a difficult fish and I'm glad I decided to rest it. Unknown to me Charles Smith had tactfully slipped away while I was trying to tempt the trout. From now on it was up to me.

I moved on upstream a short distance until I found another large fish between two weed beds. I thought it moved to my nymph the first time I threw but it certainly did not take and the next throw it ignored completely. I decided not to risk a third chance but marked the fish's position and hoped to try it again in the afternoon for it seemed to me a particularly heavy fish.

Twenty yards upstream I regained a little of my self-respect by deceiving a fish lying out in a gravelly run. It took my nymph boldly at the first throw and I hooked it well, or so I thought. Indeed I had this trout on for nearly five minutes and my net was out when it made a last rush and freed itself. The trout had simply let go as we say. The nymph had probably been hooked through a thread of skin which had frayed during the battle.

The day was wearing on and I was making no progress. Indeed, at this stage I began to wonder if I was going to catch a fish on this beat at all. Far from being depressed by this thought I was stimulated by the challenge. I stood quite still and watched the water above me intently. Thirty yards higher up I saw a big swirl as a fish undoubtedly took something beneath the surface.

I moved up to within about 15 yards of this movement and watched again, carefully, as I waited. After about 10 minutes the swirl appeared again, slightly to the left of the original spot on which my eyes were focussed. At once I got out line and threw my nymph to within a few inches of this movement. It pitched accurately and quietly and began to sink at once, and a moment later there was a movement like a pig turning round underwater. I gave the fish a second to take, for I had no doubt that the eruption beneath the surface was a voluntary acceptance of my much-delayed offer. When I struck I felt the fish's response at once as it rushed upstream. I held it hard and the trout turned and ran back towards me. I was suddenly conscious of Charles Smith standing quietly beneath the willow tree 80 yards downstream, obviously pleased to see that I was into a fish. Eventually I got the net under it and carried it back to the hut where my smiling friend congratulated me warmly on my fish. It was a perfectly proportioned trout, obviously well over 2 lb., but I had no balance with me to check this.

Charles Smith then drew my attention to a superb picnic basket which Mrs. Smith had put together for me and which he had just brought out with my host's compliments. I was also very glad to accept the loan of the bigger net which he offered me. He took away the trout to be weighed and said he would keep it cool until I had finished fishing. I sat down now to my picnic lunch with a good appetite! How sweet it all tasted, how refreshing the cool ale, drunk there in the rough comfort of the shaded fishing hut.

After lunch I went back up to the little weir just above the fishing hut and found the pale fish was moving, the one I'd failed to deceive first thing after my arrival. The nymph I had on my point, the one I'd taken my first trout on, was a rather scruffy, threadbare specimen amounting to little more than a bare oo hook, with a little fine copper wire to take it down and the last remnants of one or two pheasant tail herls.

My first cast fell right but the pale fish didn't seem to see the nymph. At all events it ignored my offer. I threw again. This time the trout half turned but did not take. I threw again and this time lifted the nymph slightly in the water. The throw was a couple of feet wide but the trout

turned aside and glided over to look at the nymph. I saw
it take quite clearly and I had quite a tussle with this fish
to prevent it tumbling over the weir. The larger net enabled
me to end the battle at the first opportunity.

Charles Smith had assured me in the morning that this
fish was well over 2 lb. In fact it proved to be 2 lb. 12 oz.
when we weighed it later, a lovely, deep, picture of a Test
trout.

The second of the two fish which had defeated me before
lunch was also lying out on the gravel higher up, and this
time it took my nymph first cast. This trout took a long
time to subdue although the fight it put up was not spec-
tacular. This was my best fish of the day and it weighed
exactly 3 lb.

During the afternoon it was quiet under the hot sun. I
found a number of nests with eggs and young along the
edge of the river. I also saw two feeding trout, each of which
betrayed its position in reflected light by bottom feeding in
such a way that its tail broke the surface. By timing my cast
to coincide with the fish levelling out, I was able to hook
them both with my first cast, each time with an induced
take. These fish later weighed 1 lb. 15 oz. and 1 lb. 14 oz.
respectively.

I took the four trout I had caught during the afternoon
back to the fishing hut where I laid them on a seat in the
shade, wrapped in their muslin fish cloths which I generally
take with me. I was thankful to ease my shoulder of the
weight and I enjoyed a bit of a rest while I had an early tea.
Then I walked up almost to the top of the beat before I
saw another fish, which I hoped to take to give me my
limit. I do not think it was a two-pounder for it took my
nymph voluntarily at the first offer and I had a good view
of it as I was about to net it. Unaccountably it let go and
bolted downstream.

A few yards above its lie I saw a swirling movement in
reflected light which seemed to me to indicate the presence
of a nice fish. I cast a few feet above it and a moment later
there was a slight acceleration at my dipping point and

when I struck, the fish splashed about violently confirming my original impression of its size. It proved to be a fish of 2 lb. 8 oz. I carried it back to the hut and put it with the others while I dismantled my tackle.

I had quite a load to carry to my car at the Mill. Just as I reached it, I met Charles Smith who was coming to see how I was faring. I think he was as delighted with my catch as I was myself. When we got back to Bere Mill, the three brace of trout together weighed 14 lb. 5 oz. I had never taken a better basket of trout or seen better fish. But they certainly had to be earned!

9

A Wet July Morning on the Upper Avon

WEDNESDAY, 12th July, 1961, was a wet day with light but continuous rain throughout the morning, accompanied by quite a strong wind. This is unpromising summer weather if your outdoor pastimes are Morris dancing, lawn tennis, and the like, but these are the conditions I prefer for fishing on the Upper Avon in July, by which time the trout of this much flogged association water vex us with their wiles, like the Midianites of old. Some of these soft showery summer days produce good and prolonged hatches of fly and plenty of lively nymphal movement under water. Fish then feed freely, much more freely than under certain apparently more pleasant conditions. Knowing this, and having the day free, I chose to take my weekly Avon day in the rain rather than wait until Saturday, my normal fishing day on this river.

I did not know whether I would succeed in catching trout but I was in no doubt that on such a morning I could certainly count on plenty of opportunities.

It was still quite early, about 9.30 a.m., but I sometimes catch trout about 8 a.m. at this time of the year, and you may even see them busy with Broadwings at sun-up. I left my car at Figheldean Bridge and crossed the meadow to Bluegate Pool at Alton Parva, disturbing the kingfisher which is often in evidence at this spot. It is sometimes difficult to locate the nest while the bird is still sitting. Once the young begin to get hungry, they soon give the site away with their curious "tractor-revving" cries.

For me Bluegate has been rather a disappointing pool as

a rule. But it was there that my daughter caught her first two fish, at the age of seven, both on the nymph. They were grayling and each weighed 1 lb. 12 oz., yet out of my last 1,500 grayling, only about half a dozen have bettered this weight! On this morning, however, some Pale Wateries were hatching on the shallows immediately below the pool and a few Blue-winged Olives were coming off in the rain as well. The fish were feeding under water and ignoring the duns, heeling and tripping before the squally wind. Most of these feeding fish seemed to be grayling and I had three of them, good fish, before I caught my first trout, all on a ragged No. o nymph.

In the rain and poor light, the wind-ruffled water made it almost impossible to see fish in the river and I had to rely on the thickly greased upper links of my cast to help me detect the takes. Fortunately in that shallow water there was usually a pronounced swirl as a fish moved to intercept my nymph.

I decided to walk farther down to Gunville hoping I might find a big trout moving in the hatch-pool. There was no one else out fishing this day; another advantage which sometimes accrues by fishing in rough wet weather. There were no big fish at Gunville but crouching by the eel trap, looking up the eddy coming from a downstream re-bound, I noticed a suggestion of movement under some trailing ranunculus close beneath the wall. When I ran the nymph down the edge of this weed there was a dull yellow gleam somewhere under water near where I judged the nymph to be, and I hit it at once: a nice pound trout.

It was at this spot about ten days later that I caught a trout of 4 lb. 8 oz. on the pheasant tail Red Spinner during the evening rise to the Blue-winged Olive and so many people came to watch, including six other rods fishing the beat at the time, that when my friend Dr. Richard Jones arrived at Crossing "C" Tank Bridge and saw them all, he assumed the worst had happened and someone had fallen in. He arrived as the fish was being netted out, expecting to begin administering artificial respiration!

9. Gunville Hatch-pool on the Upper Avon, with George Marks' Cottage on the Right.

10. "A Rough Old Place"—the Nine-mile River Nursery Stream below Sheep Bridge, Bulford.

11. The Hatch-pool on the Wylye at Fisherton-de-la-Mere.

But there were no four-pounders showing in the pool on this damp morning and I worked my way back up past the slow deep reach to the broad shallows below Bluegate again.

Below the pool, three fish were moving freely. I knelt down on the damp grass, my knees protected by my long waders—I always wear these for this reason in very wet weather—lengthened line and, casting carefully in the little lulls in the wind, caught them one after another in three casts. The first two were trout, just under a pound apiece. The third was a big grayling, a fish which had often defeated me and my friends before. Dr. Richard Jones had earlier christened it "The Pig", from the disturbance it caused when it took a natural nymph under water! Like most big grayling it was a cock fish and it weighed 1 lb. 9 oz. All three fish were easy to hook for in the thinnish water they revealed their interceptory movement by violent surface disturbance: the bow-wave indication.

A few yards higher up, at the tail of Bluegate itself, another and better trout was lying, at the end of some ranunculus over which the water was flowing in a fast rippling stream. Unlike the other fish I caught this morning, I could see this trout fairly plainly. I watched it for a moment and noticed the eagerness with which it was feeding. Although my nymph fell a foot in front of the trout when I cast, the fish took it instantly, accelerating forward and upward to do so. Fortunately my preliminary study of the trout in the water had led me to expect this and I had anticipated the take by striking as a matter of course without waiting for any indications of any kind. You get to know those situations in which you must base your actions on *a presumed take*, chiefly as a result of bitter, hard-earned experience with good fish taking nymphs and shrimps in really fast streamy runs.

At best all you see as the nymph hurtles by the fish is a short quick jerk on the trout's part that to the spectator usually goes quite unnoticed. When you hook such fish, striking for the presumed take, you tend to acquire a bogus reputation for some subtle communion with your quarry. It is nothing of the kind; just common sense. If a trout feeding in a fast rippling current went through the motions of a leisurely take with much mouth-whitening and other such indications, its intention might be clearly communicated to you, but where would it get you, and where would it get the trout, for by this time the nymph would be ten feet downstream!

Nymph fishing, I think, may be likened to deer stalking. The cast, like the actual shot, should be no more than the coup de grâce. The hard work, both the physical effort involved in the approach and the mental preparation which precedes it, is mostly done beforehand. The nymph fisher, however, has one great advantage over the stalker. Whereas the latter's hands are tied, in that his shot must take one particular trajectory, and one only, from the point at which it is fired, the nymph fisher can put his artificial almost anywhere within reasonable reach of the trout and persuade his quarry to come and get it.

This, indeed, is the very foundation of the Netheravon creed. It postulates the simple hypothesis that if you show a trout an artificial, vaguely similar in size and form to a natural but above all behaving like a natural nymph, the fish will take it as such, if you present it when it is feeding on natural nymphs of like size. There may be trout which won't, but if so, I am still looking for them. The craft of the nymph fisher takes time to acquire, however, for you must know when your nymph is taken and set the hook in the fish's jaw in the brief moment in which this is possible. The foundation of this craft is informed anticipation and this I stress again.

It is not often that fish come easy on the Upper Avon in July. On this wet morning they came very easy indeed and by this time had become a burden. I took them across the meadow and left them in the boot of my car. Needing only one more trout for my limit, I walked up above the bridge to see if I could locate a big trout known to have a lie under the ash tree around the first bend.

I could just make out the loom of my big trout under the

heaving, swishing branches of the overhanging tree. I thought I might have trouble from this tree in the wind, and, being intent on missing it with my nymph, I rather overlooked the danger from possible snags elsewhere. I was about to deliver my first cast when my nymph caught up behind me in a tall flowering reed. The fine nylon point had twisted round and round the stem many times. Although I unravelled it carefully with fingers made soft and wrinkly by the rain, the point was so badly kinked that I knew I should have to bite it off and tie on another to be on the safe side.

I hoped the fish wouldn't disappear in the meantime. Some days, when I am nymph fishing, I have a hell of a time. My nymphs catch up in branches and herbage: I once lost 11, one after another, on the broad, thickly wooded shallows above Bluegate, before I caught a fish. Fishing with Canon Robert Finch above Figheldean Mill one cold wet day, I fell in twice in the space of ten yards: into three or four feet of water. Bulls, wasps, horse-flies, barbed wire, stick-throwing women with dogs, swans, otterhounds, nettles and spilt ale—all these have attacked, provoked, tormented, irritated or otherwise annoyed me from time to time. It is right that these things should be, for without them we should never savour the sweet delights of success hard-earned.

Again I cast and my second offer was caught by the wind which slammed the nymph down cruelly into the water a good two feet beyond my trout. I saw the fish lunge forward, even as I winced myself, scared to death, no doubt, by this rough uncalled-for treatment. Not a bit: its mouth whitened momentarily, as if it half stifled a yawn. But trout don't yawn and I struck quickly, just in case my nymph was the cause of it. It was.

This fish weighed 3 lb. 2 oz. and I was back home with my limit of three brace of trout, together with two brace of grayling, within two hours of setting out. I had tried for ten fish and, with a bit of luck, had caught the lot. But would I, or anyone else, have done as well on the dry-fly that day? Who can say? I can say this. That when I examined the stomach contents of the six trout I took in, I found little evidence of hatched fly. Of course, if I'd taken in trout caught on a dry-fly it might have been different. But can you tell me where, that morning, I might have had sport on the dry-fly? Not, I think, on that part of the Upper Avon.

10

The Dog Days

WHEN you have only an occasional opportunity for fly-fishing during a season, you will be fortunate indeed if your visit coincides with a hatch of fly and you find trout moving freely on the surface. You may then enjoy fair sport on the dry-fly, if you are fond of this method. In the second half of the season, however, especially in August before fly hatches improve with the appearance of the autumn hatches in September, you may not find it easy to catch trout at all. In Chapter Thirteen is an account of nymph fishing in the River Torridge in North Devon at this time. In this chapter, I shall try to explain how to make the most of chalk-stream fishing during the dog days of August.

MAKING THE MOST OF A CHALK-STREAM DAY

Your difficulties at this time may be attributable to three main causes: either the trout are no longer there, an unhappy experience sometimes met with on artificially stocked water which has been grossly overfished and not replenished; or there are trout in the water, but they are not easy to locate, quite a common situation on even the most renowned chalk-stream fisheries in July and August; or the fish are there, you can even see them plainly enough, but either you can't get anywhere near them or you can't persuade them to take a dry-fly.

Where there are no longer any trout, the only advice I can offer is to fish somewhere else. Most of the waters I

visit at this time have no shortage of fish but I often experience the other two causes of difficulty, especially on my
home river, the Avon, which I usually fish on Saturdays
when there are generally a lot of people about and many
other rods fishing.

The river here is not difficult because of any peculiar
natural conditions. In May when the season opens it can
be positively easy and some private and under-fished reaches
not far away hold trout, wild trout, which remain relatively
suicidal throughout the season: very misleading water on
which to serve a chalk-stream apprenticeship! But during
the opening months of the trout season, so many fly-fishers
from novices to acknowledged masters from many countries
combine to remove from it nearly all the easy fish of takable
size, and the more persistent of them continue thereafter to
harry the sagacious survivors.

These remaining trout have either been pricked and lost
so many times that they have grown extremely careful as
regards the flies which they eat, both natural and artificial,
or they habitually feed in lies which, by accident or choice,
effectively protect them from being deceived by the fly-
fisher.

The problem facing you if you visit such a hard-fished
water boils down to this: to make a basket you must either
deceive wary, shy, frightened or otherwise educated trout,
or you must count on finding and catching less sophisticated
fish, like the trout described on page 83, in places which
the average competent angler tends to avoid. Typical of
these latter are lengths where overhanging trees, rank bankside herbage, or drag-producing currents make fishing exceptionally difficult. If you are an expert, fish these. If not,
you must rely on deception which calls above all for a careful
approach.

You may be fortunate if your host or a sympathetic keeper
can advise you directly on the most likely places from which
to look for worthwhile trout, especially if you are told the
probable time they will be moving and any known idiosyn-
crasies. Advice of this kind can be immensely helpful on

strange water. There are stretches of river on most fisheries
which rarely yield trout. Indeed, with the electric machine
you often find that they just don't hold any. These un-,
productive lengths may extend for 50 yards or more and
systematic observation of these parts of your beat may prove
to be a waste of valuable time. Remember that you may
have paid the best part of five pounds for your day. But it
also holds good even for welcome guests.

All credit to you if, having been given some helpful
information, you then prefer to be left alone to do the best
you can. Some people fish the better for the presence of
someone else to bring out the best of their abilities, and also
to advise them on lines of approach and means of presentation. Others tend to go to pieces if anyone is watching them,
especially if the spectator is known as a good performer himself. All credit to your informant if he gives you the opportunity you hope for. Accept the challenge but do give yourself a fair chance.

The commonest cause of failure by visiting rods on hard-
fished rivers is simply neglect to conceal their presence from
the wary trout. Consequently the game is up before they
ever begin to cast. They usually don't realise this, especially
if they are accustomed to fish easy water elsewhere, for even
wild trout have to be flogged consistently hard and carelessly
before they learn to connect anglers with mortal danger.
Once they do learn, it takes the excitements of a spawning
season to make them forget again.

A trout unaware of an angler's presence will sometimes,
though not always, take an artificial nymph which has been
delicately presented and does not drag or otherwise behave
unnaturally. If it does not, either the size is wrong, or the
fish needs its attention to be attracted to the nymph, or it is
educated, in the sullen sense of the word, perhaps having
been pricked badly a day or two earlier. A much-educated
trout, pricked into studying phenomena like drag, faulty let-
down, cast shadow, and so on, may be difficult to deceive
either on the surface or in the water and can sometimes be
seen scrutinising the naturals with the greatest care, rejecting

one after another as unacceptable risks. No fly dresser can improve on the Creator's work. Every river has, of course, its quota of trout which can eventually be deceived by a skilful caster. Ours has. They have usually all been eaten by the end of July.

Fortunately not all chalk-stream trout are as difficult to catch as all this may seem to imply. It is curious how, as the season advances, trout seem to emerge from the weed once in a while, leaving their crayfish, caddis and the like for a temporary change of diet. Sometimes after days of seeing very little moving, you come across several hard at it within a comparatively short area. Sometimes I am lucky enough to find half a dozen such fish feeding not far from one another on a reach which I am fishing. On a number of occasions this has enabled me to take a limit basket on days when rods on other parts of the river have done no good at all, having had no opportunity to put their skill to the test.

In so doing one acquires a wholly undeserved reputation for being able to charm fish under any circumstances. It isn't true: I have to work damned hard for my fish in the dog days. The great thing is to make the most of such opportunities as come your way. Unless you are exceptionally fortunate, precious few will come your way, on the Upper Avon at any rate. When they do, and you do well, the sleep of the labouring man is indeed sweet.

Trout learn to register the spots from which danger repeatedly threatens. When you visit a strange river you will generally notice that the rushes and herbage at the water's edge have been trampled into obvious gaps here and there; gaps clearly related to the lies of visible fish. Trout are well aware of these gaps and the tiresome people who regularly appear in them. They may or may not connect them with the artificial flies passing overhead but they are not insensitive to the fact that it is when these gaps are occupied, at least on bright days, that the shadows they fear are slashed into the water around them.

Pander to the timorous fish. Stop short of each treacherous gap before you begin casting to them. It requires little extra effort to throw the extra yard or two from a point slightly downstream of the much-used casting place. Always relate your approach to the available background and relate your background to the clothing you wear. Avoid clothes made from shiny material which may reflect light and alarm fish by causing flash. Do not wear light-coloured clothes unless you expect to be fishing from a high bank with little behind you except the sky. Be careful in your choice of fishing clothes. If you own a traditional willow-coloured fishing suit, you nullify the advantage it should give you if you elect to wear with it a white shirt and collar and, save the mark, a panama hat!

Against the usual background of vegetation and river-bank herbage, olive, dark khaki green, and such drab colours seem to me to be the best for fishing clothes. Some materials fade in time. A few years ago I bought a couple of dark-green shirts to begin the season with and fancied myself passing inconspicuous at the waterside. One morning in late July it was so hot that I left my jacket in my car before starting to fish. I was standing in the shade of the big chestnut tree below Choulston thinking myself pretty well camouflaged when the head keeper came up to join me, having spotted me from several hundred yards away. I had failed to realise that the shirt I was wearing had faded from sun and much laundering to a pale sage green which showed up well against my dark background.

Trout may not see colours exactly as we see them though I think they can tell light from dark. A cap helps to hide the face and may be less noticeable than a hat. I was resting on a bank seat at Syrencote one hot August after-noon in 1958 when suddenly shoals of grayling began rushing past me upstream in evident alarm, frightening the trout feeding in front of me and putting them down. Presently an old friend came quietly along the path, somewhat bowed by years and luncheon, wearing on his head a tall white straw hat which he normally affects at vicarage garden fêtes on the rare occasions when these coincide with sunshine. I am in no doubt that this refulgent souvenir of

Asquith's first term had sparked off the migration I had just witnessed.

Dress sensibly, both with regard to camouflage and to crawling about in the mud and dirt. These remarks may seem unnecessary, even bordering on impertinence, but every season I see here people trying to fish in tall hats, white jackets, suede shoes and the like. Now I have got away with this sort of thing on the padaungs of Trengganu and Alor Star but in Wiltshire in the dog days it simply blights the prospects, certainly of the wearer, perhaps of others as well.

Remember that a good many of the fish which feed in full view during the latter part of the season are notorious Aunt Sallies, especially those, both trout and grayling, whose lies are adjacent to popular car parking sites and at the junctions between beats. Many fishermen, particularly the less skilled, conscious of their empty baskets, feel impelled to have a chuck at them, both when they arrive to start fishing and when they knock off to eat their sandwiches, or to go home in despair complaining about sullen trout.

To be able to fish well is no more reprehensible than to be able to write legibly or to drink soup without slobbering. To hear some people talk, it might be inferred that to be able to chuck a fly or nymph, deceive a fish, hook and speedily kill or release it were arty-crafty accomplishments somewhat beneath the dignity of the initiated. Now we all make far too many mistakes in fishing but, after all, we fish for recreation not as a precision exercise. But this does not absolve each one of us from fishing to the best of our individual ability. Fish are living creatures, after all, and I for one am sensitive of the hurt I may cause them even when I am trying my hardest. To fish carelessly is inhuman; criminally so.

If you can cast effectively backhanded or, better still, if you are left-handed, choose the left bank of the river (looking downstream) because the fish under that bank may be, and generally are, less educated than those under the right bank. If there are trees close behind the left bank, so that merely awkward casting becomes downright difficult, this will almost certainly be the case. But do not elect to fish in such places if you are completely out of practice, or have a weak wrist, otherwise casting becomes a labour and the constant snagging and knot tying very tedious.

If you are right out of practice after a long illness or spell abroad, in gaol or in towns, it might be better to select a likely looking piece of water and concentrate on studying it carefully for signs of feeding fish. Look under the banks rather than in the middle, except where the nymph-laden currents divide and flow through the weed bars. These positions are generally tenanted by good trout which can sometimes be caught off balance with a carefully judged first throw.

If you really are short of practice, don't rely on getting it on the water you've been asked to fish. Try and put in an hour or so loosening up either on grass or water. A big lawn, tennis court, park or even garage or hangar would do at a pinch. A pond or sailing boat enclosure is even better. I often use either an open-air swimming pool or static water pool, for I reckon to be out of practice if I go more than three or four days without fishing.

Unless you see fish actually taking natural insects on the surface, think in terms of nymph fishing during the day time, reserving the dry-fly for relaxation during the evening rise. Do not be unduly discouraged if through age or infirmity you are unable to cover long stretches of the river in quest of nymphing trout. Many such rods of my acquaintance more than hold their own with younger and more active men by taking up a quiet observation position from which they can watch the river. Although they may only spot a few trout rising during the course of a long day, by approaching them carefully and making their first cast tell, they can usually count on returning home with a brace or so.

Never be scared by a river's reputation. Plenty of people who fish the Avon regularly have never caught a two-pounder. Plenty more have not caught two. Yet a couple of years ago the great Swedish fly-fisher, Nils Färnström, came to Figheldean and took a brace of two-pounders on his first day. But he had been careful to take the trouble to master the Netheravon style in his own country first, under Sawyer's personal instruction.

OLIVE SPINNERS AND SOME MORNING TACTICS

Olive spinners lay their eggs under water, choosing well-aerated sites which are easily accessible from above. Thus on a rough river they settle on boulders and stones which project above the water and crawl down them to lay beneath the surface. On the chalk-streams the piers and abutments of bridges and hatches provide easy access to suitable laying sites and these places are consequently much favoured by Olive spinners throughout the season.

Large trout often elect to make their homes in the masonry crevices beneath bridges and also under tree roots and in holes in the banks flanking deep hatch-pools. These fish may only rarely be seen and their size may be much above the average for the water. One of the best chances of finding such a fish on the feed in August occurs during the morning when Olive spinners may be descending to lay in great numbers. These spinners are most plentiful after good hatches of duns have taken place during the preceding days, perhaps in damp weather, and when the morning is quiet enough to enable them to reach the water unhampered by strong winds or heavy rain.

The biggest of the trout feed on the spinners by picking them off the masonry as they are crawling down it to their laying sites. The stonework is usually coated with algae or dark-green moss-like vegetation and these trout appear to the observer to be browsing on this greenstuff whereas they are in fact taking spinners below the water line.

A large trout may feed purposefully in this way, quietly moving up and down the moss line along a pier or abutment wall as it does so. The constant action of picking the adult flies off the rough stone, brickwork or concrete wears the edges of the trout's jaws, leaving whitish scars on them. These scars show up in the water and may sometimes betray the trout, disclosing its movements in conditions of poor visibility.

Less powerful fish may be unable to command a place along the browsing line and may have to be content with lies just downstream of the piers where they can intercept spent spinners surfacing as they drift away from their laying sites on completion of their brief purpose. It may be necessary to remove these lesser fish before tackling the real prize, the big browsers, otherwise the smaller trout may be alarmed by a line cast over their heads direct to the larger fish. This would cause them to rush forward and scare the main quarry.

If you fish smallish rivers, where trout are perhaps numerous but really good ones are few and far between, these tactics must be worked out systematically and applied with care. I have found them invaluable in streams like the little Ebble in South Wiltshire and in the small carriers of large chalk-streams.

The manner of removing lesser fish depends on the depth at which they are feeding. If they are taking mostly spent fly in the surface film, a spinner pattern may be employed. If the fish are feeding below the surface, mainly on drifting nymphs and larvae, and taking an occasional spent spinner, a quick-sinking nymph is likely to be accepted if presented at the appropriate depth. I say appropriate because I dislike the term "correct". There is something mandatory about it.

Trout hooked below hatches generally turn downstream towards the hatch-pool quite voluntarily because, more often than not, their hides are there. When they obligingly do this, there is less danger of them alarming fish in the hatchways above.

Outliers below bridge piers often react in the opposite way. They usually try to make upstream to the shelter of the arches and in cases like these must be restrained from doing so with some care lest they give the game away.

Once the lesser trout have been taken care of, the capture of the larger fish above may be a relatively simple matter. You stand a reasonable chance of catching it off guard when its attention is focussed just beneath the surface during the course of active feeding along the moss line. A little nymph, as near a bare hook as you've got, pitched gently in front of an advancing fish may be quietly snapped up by the unsuspecting trout and if your nerves are equal to the task of setting the hook, you can expect a vigorous reaction.

One way of dropping the nymph close to the fish's feeding line is to cast it lightly, taking full advantage of any favourable wind, against the pier or abutment about a foot or more above the water. The nymph is then allowed to drop gently just in front of the advancing fish. It is an added advantage if this can be done as the trout is working downstream towards you. It will then be less likely to be scared by the cast or its shadow and you will be well placed to look your gift horse full in the mouth. Don't panic as that mouth whitens but remember to strike as the whiteness shutters off.

Don't try to play this game according to a set procedure. Take advantage of any circumstances which may enable you to get on good terms with your quarry. At Choulston there is a bit of a ledge just above the water-line and I sometimes lay point and nymph on this, easing them off at the critical moment to drop the nymph almost into the mouth of an advancing browser.

Once a browser becomes aware of your presence, your chances of taking it are much reduced. Indeed, these large, shy, wild trout may go down for the day once they are disturbed by fishermen or passers-by. On Saturday mornings when I fish the Avon there are usually a number of people about, including many children who like to peer over the bridges, as we ourselves do. I therefore like to get out early as soon as I have had breakfast, even before breakfast at times. Having found a fish, an accurate first cast is of paramount importance.

HOW STOCK FISH VIEW THE NYMPH

In 1960 and 1961, the Officers' Fishing Association boosted the native population of big trout in the Upper Avon with

50 stock fish, turned in here and there in small numbers in likely holding water. These stock fish were introduced each year after the Mayfly ended in June. They formed only a small part of the total trout population for we catch an average of about 1,500 trout a season; sometimes over 2,000. And with 75 members and their guests fishing, the proportion worked out at one between two rods at best. Until 1960 the river had not been stocked for 30 years by the O.F.A. I believe there is much to be said for the experiment. It gave members the chance to catch a really big trout, even in the dog days. And it gave us all a fair chance of doing so, whether we were in form and practice or not.

Towards the end of July 1960, I had my friend Billy Walmsley of Blackburn staying with me at Netheravon. When Saturday morning came, I had my usual preliminary chat with the head keeper, Frank Sawyer, before going out to fish, accompanied by my guest. Frank said that one of the large stock fish had been showing just above one of the bridges shortly before eleven o'clock each morning. I ought to catch it, he thought, at about ten minutes to eleven. He proposed to come along at five-to and confirm that it was a two-pounder. In the event he arrived at ten minutes to, just after my friend had netted the trout out for me. It weighed 2 lb. 2 oz.

I hadn't been able to see the fish in the river although I had kept a careful watch for it. Something had moved in a midstream pocket of deeper water in reflected light a little way above the bridge. It was a complicated cast owing to the waterside trees, necessitating an upstream delivery followed by a roll cast to take the nymph out to midstream. This was accomplished, however, and the nymph seemed to be presented just right. Nothing happened. Before it was too late, I imparted pronounced lift to the nymph, there was a swirl and a large trout previously quite invisible to me swung round to hunt it downstream. I saw the tell-tale check of the dipping point as the fish took and turned and my strike set the hook firmly.

If you can find large stock fish feeding under water, little skill is required to catch them until they, too, have been harried and hammered into caution. Even the timing of the strike is much less difficult than it is in the case of wild fish. Among the stock fish put into the Upper Avon in 1961 were some quite large trout up to 4 lb. or so in weight. We had not ordered these but they had been supplied because fish of more modest proportions were apparently in short supply.

Our honorary secretary, Colonel Alan Lane, was naturally concerned to ensure that these larger trout did not survive too long to become predatory menaces in the fishery, and he asked me to do what I could to catch some of the big ones after July 1st. Some of the larger fish, I had been told, had been put into the river by the hatchery in the meadow behind my cottage. There I went after breakfast on July 1st, for ever honoured in the East Lancashire Regiment, as in others, as Somme Day.

Sure enough, there were several good trout showing on the bend. I could see them quite clearly as I knelt 12 yards downstream behind a screen of meadowsweet. They were feeding about a foot under the surface in a manner which left me in no doubt that I could be reasonably sure of taking my pick and deceiving it. Now hatchery fish have a lot to learn about food creatures, whether nymphs, duns, shrimps or anything else. Some may never learn, and waste away. If food supplies are plentiful, as in the Avon, they do very well, as I shall presently confirm beyond doubt. They also learn discretion in time, or die. A good many are caught, of course—we couldn't afford to put them in if this were not so—but if you imagine all stock fish remain suicidal to the end of their days, buy yourself some sobering experience at Leckford, say, about August time.

But this was July 1st and I chose my fish carefully, picking the biggest of about four. I pitched my oo nymph into the slow-flowing water about a yard upstream of it so that it almost brushed the big trout's mouth as it reached it. The trout ignored the nymph completely, as might have been expected: if it had been pellet-shaped it might have obliged with a voluntary take but that would not be nymph fishing.

12. A LEASH OF TEST TROUT BETWEEN 2½ AND 3 LB., TAKEN BY THE AUTHOR AT POLHAMPTON MILL ON 6TH JUNE 1961.

13. The Shallows above Bluegate Pool on the Avon at Alton Parva.

But the moment I used the rod tip to move the nymph a few inches in the water, as much laterally as upward, the fish turned broadside on to seize it with savage eagerness, looking like an aquatic airship, if that isn't too much of a contradiction in terms. It weighed 4 lb. 1 oz.

It was during that same morning, when I was fishing in reflected light, that another large stock fish took my nymph. I hadn't known it was there and when I saw it turn into the take, I deliberately held my hand so as not to hook it, for I had no wish to take home two tame fish in a day. It began to look as if the fish would insist on hooking itself. It swam slowly past me downstream, then swung round facing upstream and lying close to the bottom in about four feet of water. I pulled off slack line, hoping the action of the current on the cast would not hook the trout. I then quietly laid my rod down on the bank beside me. After several minutes the stock fish swam slowly back upstream to its original feeding lie, lifted in the water and then, and not until then, seemed to become aware of the pull exerted on the cast by the current. With a jerk of its head and some visible mouth snapping, conveyed to me by repeated whitening beneath the glassy surface, the trout succeeded in ejecting the nymph and I was able to reel up and pass on to smaller but more sophisticated quarry.

We mark our stock fish so that rods can identify them and report details of any they catch. We use a different mark each season. Soon after the 1961 season opened in May, Dr. Fleming brought a nicely conditioned two-pounder to my house. He had caught the fish that afternoon at Figheldean and I recognized it from the marking as one of the stock fish we had turned in early in June 1960. Later in the month, Colonel Pat Badham of the 3rd Carabiniers caught another trout of the 1960 batch near the Bailey Bridge at Crossing "C". This was a much bigger fish of over 3¼ lb. I mention these captures because it is sometimes said that stock fish cannot maintain themselves when turned into a river. These could, and did. It all depends on the river.

★ I I ★

A Sunny August Day on Plunket Greene's Bourne

THE last day of August 1961 was delightful. The morning began with a slight mist, soon dispelled by the warm sunshine though its legacy of heavy dew persisted until late in the morning. My friend, Captain Michael Kelton, with whom I had fished the Bourne earlier in the season, was himself away in Scotland shooting at the time but had kindly invited me to have another day. I had therefore been in touch with Major Frank Schwind who has charge of the water. He himself has fished the Bourne for over 30 years and seems to know most of the trout in it. I was therefore grateful for his advice about where to fish and the time to begin.

As I drove over from Netheravon on that late-summer morning, I looked forward to my day on the Bourne with the keenest possible anticipatory pleasure. I took the Whitchurch road from Andover with a feeling close, I fancy, to that experienced by pilgrims in the Middle Ages as they approached the shrines of saints. At the bottom of Hurstbourne hill I turned left, passing the attractive cricket ground, then right, to park my car in the shade of the trees by the church.

I lost no time putting my tackle together: 8 ft. 6 in. glass rod, 10 ft. cast with a yard of fine nylon on the point, a well stocked fly box in one pocket and, of course, the little pink nymph box still containing a few remnants, sharpened up for the occasion, in the other. Then I turned my back on the quiet churchyard where, a stone's throw from the river he loved so well, rests Harry Plunket Greene, the most famous Bourne fly-fisher of all.

I crossed the bottom meadow, where there were mushrooms in the dewy grass, to the Cascades, an attractive, thickly wooded short reach comprising several small waterfalls. There were one or two nice trout lying out in the water immediately above the Cascades but they seemed desperately shy and difficult to approach.

The Bourne hereabouts is completely open on the right or Hurstbourne bank. The river is very clear and quite shallow in places while its average width is probably about six yards. Plunket Greene wrote charmingly of this winsome stream, its golden gravel and bright green weed beds, and his favourite fly, the little Iron Blue, tripping along the surface down towards the Whitchurch road.

Few Iron Blues seem to hatch from the Bourne today but great trout still lie in the gravel runs between the starwort clumps and celery beds and in shallow water of limpid clarity tax the skill of the fly-fisher to the utmost.

This is as it should be for by the end of August the nymph fisherman should be at the peak of his form. Beginning with odd days in June, perhaps earlier some years, he should have had plenty of practice all through July to perfect his technique for without it, his prospects of being consistently successful on really hard-fished chalk-stream waters, strange as well as familiar, would not be at all bright.

Trout in the open water could not see my approach, as long as I was careful and did not try to get too near, but as soon as I cast, the shadow of the fine point on the gravel sent them darting for cover. I knew I was going to have to earn my fish this day, and that is how I like it. If they won, it would be good experience. If I won, it would be very satisfying. I didn't think they would win, but you can never be sure. If you think you can, you should be writing this, not reading it.

I reached a point a little way downstream of a few trees which shaded the water beneath them. I could see a good trout feeding under water in this short, shaded length. I watched it for some time, turning first one way then the other, lifting and dipping in the water as it intercepted food particles drifting to it from a bed of water-celery just above it. I felt sure this trout would take a nymph provided I took care to ensure that it did not see the cast. The trees helped by reducing the chance of shadow.

But first I tried the fish with the dry-fly: Iron Blue, to start with, if only as a gesture to the Bourne's great chronicler; getting no response I followed with an Olive Dun, then that powerful extractor, the pheasant-tail Red Spinner. When that, too, was refused, I knew it was to be the nymph or nothing.

I threw a fairly long line, crouched low at the water's edge, and allowed my cast to recoil slightly on the backlash to pitch the nymph into the water a foot to the right of the trout and on a level with its tail. As I expected, and hoped, the fish immediately swung round and took the nymph quite viciously. It was a simple matter in these circumstances to set the hook. The trout weighed 1 lb. 6 oz.

It was some time before I got another one. I came to a length of fast-flowing water where the stream was flanked on the opposite side by hurdles set in the water. There were two nice fish in this bit, one in mid-stream and one rather farther up, close to the hurdles themselves. The mid-stream fish seemed active enough in the water, I could see its tail going well.

I cast my little nymph (00 hook—bright day, shy trout) expecting a voluntary take. I didn't get one. I offered a second time; again no response. I lengthened line a little for the third cast: this fish needed a bit of persuasion. As the nymph approached the fish, clearly visible to me in the pellucid stream, I lifted it slightly in the water with my rod tip. I saw the fish lift slightly too, nothing else, but it was enough. I felt for it quickly and was rewarded with a firm pull as the fish ran hard upstream.

This was a better fish than the first, pulling the balance down to 1½ lb. Thinking that the fish lying near the hurdles might have been disturbed by this performance, I waited for a few minutes before trying it, refreshing myself with an apple I'd put in my pocket before leaving the car, and taking in the quiet beauty of the valley. There was a touch of mellow colour already in the old elms and the chestnut tree in the park was quite richly tinted, yet in a thorn bush on the opposite bank I had earlier disturbed a sitting woodpigeon.

Not one single dun did I see hatch throughout the morning. I examined a bit of starwort from the water beside me. It was full of freshwater shrimps and young snail, superb trout food, but of nymphs I saw no sign, though this was not a serious search.

When I could see the fish under the hurdle moving quite freely, I threw my nymph upstream, a couple of feet to the left of its head to avoid cast shadow, and it turned out to take at the first offer. This trout had a healed heron stab on its back, but it was a young fish with plenty of growth in it still so I gently twitched it free and it swam away smartly enough, once it got the hang of the idea.

The long field below the road bridge which I was now approaching is aptly named Buttercup Meadow. It is a blaze of gold in late May. Towards the top of this reach there was a really good trout in a pocket of deeper water close to some tree roots. This fish I also hooked and returned unharmed.

It was now about 2 p.m. and the hot sunshine made me think longingly of the cool ale in my car. I left the river at the bridge to walk back down the road towards Hurstbourne and my car at the church. Frank Schwind had very kindly promised to come out in the afternoon and show me the lies of some goodish fish. I met him halfway back to Hurstbourne. He hadn't a lot of time to spare and I decided to postpone my lunch, and the ale, so that I could take full advantage of his offer.

He showed me a place above the bridge, near the fishing hut, where he thought I might find a big one later on, then drove me up to a field he called Chicken Meadow, towards the top of the water. We left the car and walked down this

meadow to a point from which he led me cautiously to the
water's edge. There, in fair view, was the first trout he
wished me to try for, a good trout and feeding too, under
water. I hooked it first throw and felt the first kick of pleasure
before I blotted my copybook by losing the fish in the weed.

At the bottom of Chicken Meadow he produced another
nice fish. This one, also, I deceived first time. It took with
an obvious enough whitening of the mouth, but although I
was expecting this and struck at once, for some unaccountable reason the hook didn't take hold and I never even
touched the fish. I think it may have had it half taken between slightly curved jaws and lost it without a prick as I
struck, as hissed words come from the corner of an old-time
film gangster's mouth. At any rate it's as good an excuse as
I've been able to think up. No amount of delicacy and persuasion would tempt this trout to come again, and I gave it
best.

Farther down, under some willows, there were two really
big trout, in lies perhaps 50 yards apart. Both were dormant
and refused to look at anything. A pity, for one, especially,
was clearly an outstanding trout, for any water. Indeed I
heard from Frank Schwind a few weeks later, when he caught
it himself, that it was well over 3 lb.

My companion then suggested that I might like to try the
Bourne rivulet, the fork of the river which comes down from
beneath the railway viaduct. I had often looked down on
this tiny stream when crossing the viaduct in the London
train. Now, at the end of August, the rivulet was scarcely
more than eight feet wide at its broadest. It flowed in
gravelly runs about knee-deep between great tresses of
ranunculus and starwort clumps.

While I was fishing it up as far as the viaduct, the top
boundary of the water, Major Schwind went on ahead
round the road. I got about halfway up the rivulet reach
before I spotted a fish, a solid trout lying on a little shelf
of bright gravel close under the left bank, the bank I was on
myself. Before I engaged the fish I had a close look round
for bulls. There weren't any this day.

The last day I'd fished the Bourne, I'd come this way and had got thus far when I looked up to see a bull lumbering across the field. I prepared to defend myself with my rod butt, but needn't have bothered, the animal just wanted to drink, after which it sloped off to its cows contentedly enough and I decided on a tactical withdrawal in case it should change its mind.

Casting backhanded I was lucky enough to drop the nymph into the gravel pocket only an inch or two in front of the trout. It took at once. Although I couldn't see its jaws, I saw it lift slightly but very quickly the moment the nymph pitched in and I hit it as it levelled out again. It was a lovely wild Bourne trout of $1\frac{3}{4}$ lb.

After an uncomfortable and unsuccessful stalk to try and reach a fish lying just above a fence under the viaduct itself, we drove back to Hurstbourne church, arriving there about 4.30 p.m. My companion left me then, expressing the hope that I would find one or two big ones at home up by the hut later on. I slaked my now very considerable thirst and ate a bit of late lunch. I don't go in for elaborate lunches, as my friends know very well: a small tin of sardines, a handful of lettuce leaves, perhaps stiffened with something I pick up hard by—a few dandelion leaves, garlic spears or sprigs of watercress—a crust of dry bread, black coffee and, if I want it, a flagon of ale. Time enough for unimportant things like eating when I get back home.

Before I went back up to the bridge, taking the car this time, I had another look at the bit above the Cascades where I hadn't been able to get near the trout in the morning. A darkish fish lying on the gravel came across a couple of feet in response to a very long throw and as it was past its best I killed it. Then I went back to the car and drove up to the bridge.

As Frank Schwind had said, there were some nice fish in this bit. The first I saw was close under the right bank along which I was quietly moving. I was rather close to it before I spotted it, but with a certain amount of background from trees and bushes my approach had evidently not registered on the fish. I dropped my nymph just ahead of it and a little to its right. As it turned and lifted slightly to take, its jaws whitened and the combination of the two indications made hooking easy.

This fish did not run but thrashed about violently more or less in one place, like a big December grayling. It was still flailing away as I drew it carefully over my net: an older fish, 1 lb. 10 oz. This fish was a good example of how easy quite a big and experienced trout can be to catch, in difficult water on a difficult day, if you happen across it when the dice are heavily loaded in your favour.

I saw a number of other trout whose weight I put at between 1¼ and 1½ lb., but did not cast to them as I felt certain I should see a bigger one sooner or later and I rather wanted to make up my three-brace limit with a 2-pounder, if possible.

Near the top of this rather wooded reach I came across three good fish lying fairly close together in a pocket on the gravel where a patch of sunlight hampered my vision a little. I decided to rely on my dipping point to tell me when my nymph was taken. I cast delicately to where I thought the best of the fish would be well placed to intercept my nymph. Almost at once there was a short tug at the dipping point and my strike sent a powerful trout haring off up the gravelly shallows and the two others which had been lying handy went off downstream, giving me what I took to be sullen glances as they went by. Depend on it, trout can be very expressive creatures, if you sense how they feel!

The fish I had hooked was a bonny fighter and when I netted it at last I was pleased to find it go exactly 2 lb. on the balance. My six fish this day weighed 2 lb., 1 lb. 12 oz., 1 lb. 10 oz., 1 lb. 8 oz., 1 lb. 6 oz. and 1 lb. 5 oz., a total of 9 lb. 9 oz. Most were taken first throw and it may seem odd that in my diary I confess that I found this a rather difficult day. But it was, and although I took some nice trout, there were others which I failed even to get near, and others again which just weren't feeding and gave me no chance of deceiving them.

These sun-bright, low-water, late-summer chalk-stream conditions can be quite testing even when one is in regular practice. In the previous ten days, for example, I had fished the Wylye twice and the Avon, in Wiltshire, and the Test, Anton and Itchen in Hampshire. This was the only day I described in my diary as difficult. It is significant that apart from this day on the Bourne, only two of the many trout I caught in this period were taken on the nymph. Even the grudging Avon had yielded me a handsome three brace on the 24th, all on the pheasant-tail Red Spinner during a rise to the Blue-winged Olive in the afternoon. But then trout are usually easy to catch, given plenty of Blue-winged Olives. On the Bourne this day I had seen none, and no other duns of any kind, for that matter.

It would not have been at all difficult to have had a complete blank on this particular day, despite the visible presence of plenty of sizeable trout in this delightful fishery. To fish this charming water, however, is a rare privilege, and even a blank day in the peace and beauty of Hurstbourne Priors, where surely the spirit of Plunket Greene still moves on the bright waters, would leave one with a store of pleasant memories.

★ I2 ★

A Stormy September Day on the Wylye

I ATTENDED the annual General Meeting of the Wiltshire Fisheries Association which was held in Salisbury on Thursday 14th September 1961. The business of the meeting was completed in the morning, and after lunch the other members and I drove over to Stockbridge to see something of the Test fishery of the famous Houghton Club.

We were shown round by Mr. Alfred Lunn and his son and afterwards visited the Club's room in the Grosvenor Arms. It was a delightful sunny September day and after we had been taken to see one of the beats on the river, I walked back to the Grosvenor with Wing Commander James Everidge of Bishopstrow, near Warminster. He very kindly invited me to have a day's fishing on the Wylye as his guest, and offered me the choice of a Wilton Club beat at the lower end of the valley or the Marquess of Bath's water on the upper Wylye. I had never fished the latter and having, at Mayfly time earlier in the season, had a most enjoyable day on the Wilton Club water with Sir John Paskin, I elected for the upper Wylye which was available next day.

The location and boundaries of Lord Bath's water were already known to me. The Wing Commander explained the rules and said he would leave it to me to begin anywhere I chose within the boundaries of the fishery. He suggested that I should limit my basket to three brace, if I could get them, and asked me to let him know in due course how I fared.

The next day was undoubtedly one of the most unpleasant I ever tried to fish in. Heavy rain fell continuously all the time I was out and a strong wind, blowing directly downstream, freshened to gale force by the time I started fishing. I have a note in my diary that as a result of it, a number of lives were lost in various parts of the country that day and the next.

I reached the river at Longbridge Deverill soon after 11 a.m., parked my car not far from the main bridge over the Wylye, and quickly put on my waterproof fishing coat and rubber boots. I then went to have a preliminary look over the bridge. It was difficult to see anything in the wind-torn, rain-lashed water. Leaves, twigs and other debris swirled past me in the wind, combining with the rain drops to sting my cheeks and make my eyes smart. I did not find it easy to persuade myself that there was any point in putting my tackle together to begin fishing at all. So late in the season, however, I realised that if I forfeited this opportunity to fish this water which had long attracted me, I could hardly expect to receive another. I was comforted too by the knowledge that there had been plenty of wet windy days during the course of the 1961 season and none of them had proved blank.

To give myself the best chance of competing with the conditions I selected my stiffest fibre-glass rod, a No. 4 line and a cast shortened to eight feet six inches with a point only two feet six inches long. Appreciating that there was little likelihood of fish being able to feed on the surface in so violent a wind, I tied on a well-wired nymph on a No. 1 hook and greased all of my cast except the point with a generous application of mucilin, both to keep it afloat and to make it more visible in the choppy water.

I studied the wide shallows just above the bridge as best I could. Despite the weather, occasional Blue-winged Olives were coming up and being quickly whirled away by the wind. I saw no fish rising but now and again I thought I detected movements beneath the surface in the thin water both in the gravelly runs between the weed and under my own bank.

In the clear shallow water, scarcely deep enough to cover the fish's dorsal fins, it was very difficult indeed to get near them and the gale made long casting absolutely out of the question. When at last I did hook an 11-inch fish, I didn't hesitate to put it into my basket, feeling that it had been harder earned than some 2-pounders taken earlier in the season.

It was more than an hour before I got another, a rather bigger fish, in the slightly exposed water downstream of the road bridge at Hill Deverill. A better fish lying in the shelter of a pier in relatively calm water almost under the bridge looked a sitting target, but when I cast to it, the wind held the nymph so that it dropped a good two feet behind the trout. The fish swung round, hunted it back confidently enough, and was about to take it when it became aware of my presence and was off like a flash.

Above the bridge the Wylye narrows and the top boundary of Lord Bath's water is located just around the first bend. In this short headwater stretch is a length of fairly deep water, sheltered to some extent by a tall hedge on one bank. This slow-flowing reach, which has an average depth of three to four feet, shelves to a gravelly shallow supporting a growth of ranunculus immediately above the little bridge itself. From the bridge I could just make out the loom of a good trout lying in fast-streaming water on the gravel between some ranunculus growing on the shallows ten yards upstream.

I moved quietly down on to the bank path and crawled forward as close as I dared to within feasible casting distance. From my position behind a tussock on the bank I could see that the trout would probably take my nymph, for its tail was moving and there was no tell-tale curl of its dorsal fin, always a sure sign that a trout is aware of one's approach.

I cast my nymph with my rod held low so as not to alarm the fish. Again the wind checked the cast and the nymph dropped into the river accurately enough for line but only a few inches ahead of the trout. Although I saw nothing to indicate that the fish had taken it, a take in these circumstances was an almost certain assumption and I struck quickly, for the presumed take. But I was not quick enough. The trout had taken the nymph all right and had probably begun to eject it before my strike could register effectively. I just touched the fish and turned it over, as we say, without hurting it or alarming it unduly. Somewhat puzzled, the trout swam slowly forward and disappeared into the cover of some ranunculus a few yards farther upstream.

In the deeper water about 15 yards higher up I noticed a long raft of old weed which had collected and lodged beneath the opposite bank. The cover which this afforded on the edge of a likely holding reach promised well. I studied the weed raft carefully and thinking a fish might be lying under a projection about two thirds of the way down, I cast my nymph to test the theory. A small trout flashed out to take it. I held my hand while the fish ejected it, took again, ejected a second time and backed slowly downstream looking at the nymph in obvious amazement and disbelief. I withdrew it before it could take it again and this time threw considerably higher so that the nymph would be well sunk beneath the surface by the time it reached the top edge of the weed raft. In the dismal conditions and choppy water at that point I was obliged to watch my thickly greased cast for an indication of a take. Sure enough, as it drew level with the edge of the weed raft the white cast checked in its trough in the wavelets. I felt for the fish at once: a sharp flick, not a groping movement. The trout was on and tore downstream past me pulling vigorously on the arc of line. The fish fought well to the end and when I finally netted it out I had an idea that it might be a 2-pounder, but weighed on accurate scales later it proved to be 2 oz. short of this.

It was now about 2 p.m. and I was ready for a break. I squelched off down the road to Longbridge Deverill, turned right at the cross roads and went on over the bridge where I had begun to the place where I had parked my car. I was so wet and there was so much rain running off me that I thought it best not to get into it at this stage. It was impossible to keep the rain off my piece of bread so I ate a modest lunch consisting of a tin of sardines and half a bottle of ale. Then I took off my sodden cap, gave my face and head a good rub with the dry towel from the boot of my car, put my cap back on, off-loaded my leash of trout and went back to the river to try and get the other three.

I decided this time to take a look below the bridge. I walked down the bank path past the shallows, through someone's chicken run, and out into a meadow beside a fairly deep slow-flowing reach. The wind seemed to be playing strange tricks here. Patches of smooth water unaccountably occurred among racing waves, though every now and again flurries of wind, of some violence, changed the patterns of the surface. I thought I could see a trout lying in deep water under some overhanging bushes on the far bank but it was a long time before the surface conditions enabled me to confirm the impression. Once I did I had the fish first chuck, and a solid trout it proved to be, weighing 1 lb. 5 oz.

Some way farther down the meadow I saw two trout, a few yards apart, lying close to the bottom in rather deep water. They seemed to be resting and this impression was confirmed when I failed to interest either of them in a nymph presented respectably enough at their own level.

For a long time the violence of the wind gave me a lot of trouble among the willows along the shallow reaches below this meadow. I broke my point and retied it many times and my only reward from this very exposed water was one trout of a modest 11 inches. On one shallow and rather wide length I deceived quite a decent trout which I failed to hook and after I had turned it over rather violently the fish disappeared upstream. On such a day chances of this kind should not have been allowed to pass unaccepted. The conditions are no excuse for squandering opportunities, not in September.

I made my way back up to the deeper water in the meadow, alternatively observing and moving on a few yards, hoping to locate a worthwhile trout to make up my limit. The keeper joined me there. He commiserated with me on the weather, and I with him, and I showed him the brace of fish in my bag. He was pleased to know that I had enjoyed some interesting sport in these unpromising conditions.

He left me then to carry on with his work lower down and I squelched back up to the bridge without seeing anything more. On the bridge itself I met Wing Commander Everidge who had very kindly come out to check whether I had braved the weather and to see if there was anything I wanted. He was pleased with my catch which I showed him and urged me to try and take another brace while I was at it. I told him I would be more than content if I could get one more trout to make up my target of three brace, thanked him for my testing and enjoyable day and promised to drop him a card listing the details of my basket.

I made my way quietly up the path between the two bridges. I was hoping very much that my friend had resumed his lie on the shallows above the top bridge—the fish I had failed to hook on the presumed take just before lunch.

He had. He weighed exactly 1½ lb. and his mouth was full of freshwater shrimps. And when we dressed him, he cut red, like a salmon.

My basket on this unpromising day, all taken on nymph, consisted of trout weighing 1 lb. 14 oz., 1 lb. 8 oz., 1 lb. 5 oz., 10 oz., 10 oz., and 9 oz., total 6 lb. 8 oz. The three big fish were all red-fleshed, as red as any I've caught on any chalkstream anywhere. Fish from the upper Test and Plunket Greene's Bourne share this noticeable characteristic. There is something about the headwaters of these Wessex chalkstreams which produces truly superb trout.

If ever there was a day when the dry-fly would have been unrewarding, it was this one. Rain, and wind too, are often conducive to excellent sport on the dry-fly. But in storm conditions, at this time of the year, I think you either fish the nymph or go home troutless to the substitute comforts of a hot bath and dry linen.

★ 13 ★

Torridge Interludes

RINGING THE CHANGES

ALTHOUGH most of my fishing is nowadays done in the chalk-stream area where I have lived and worked most of the time since 1955, I try to obtain some variety each year by fishing in other and quite different surroundings. In this year, 1962, for example, I am planning to open on the Teifi and Usk in Wales in March; to fish the Ribble and Hodder, my old home rivers, when I am spending Easter with my mother in Lancashire in April: to spend a week-end fishing the Charentonne, Avre and Risle in Normandy in May, as the guest of Monsieur Jean Chevalier who is himself coming to fish with me in Wiltshire on his way home from Scotland earlier in the month; and to have a few days with Colonel John Bade in Norway in July, if I can get away. Top priority for 1963, if I am spared, is the Aberdeenshire Don.

It is, I think, an advantage to pick up most of one's outside experience the hard way, fishing, as I have mostly done, on hotel and association waters where there are often fish to spare if, but only if, you can adapt your technique to local conditions.

One of my favourite hotel waters is at Woodford Bridge between Holsworthy and Bideford in North Devon. The Woodford Bridge Hotel is an attractive, whitewashed, thatched inn kept by an expert fly-fisher, Commander J. S. Douglas, R.N., and has about four miles of good trout water on the Torridge beside which the hotel stands in its own delightful gardens.

14. Choulston Bridge and Hatch-pool, Netheravon.

15. The Marquess of Bath's Water on the Upper Wylye at Job's Mill.

I fished this water on three occasions in the 1960 and 1961 seasons. In one instance, at the opening of the 1961 season in mid-March, sport was good on the dry-fly throughout my stay, as it was on the Tamar and Otter which I also fished at that time, and I did not employ the artificial nymph at all throughout my stay in the South West from 15 to 19 March.

The previous year I stayed at Woodford Bridge in early May and fished the Torridge from 7 to 12 May inclusive. On the first three days the Hawthorn-fly was much in evidence and the artificial Hawthorn-fly, fished dry, gave me all the sport I wanted. But then, its brief season being over, I had to fish below the surface to interest the trout.

The Torridge at Woodford Bridge comprises a series of long quiet pools up to four feet deep, at the time of my May 1960 visit, connected by fast shallow runs over loose stones and shillets some of which have scoured deeper holes here and there. There is not much weed: a few patches of water-celery, especially in shallow, partially exposed places in mid-stream, and occasional ranunculus tresses, shorter and altogether less luxuriant than the chalk-stream growth.

The nymphs of a number of upwinged flies are to be found in the river including Mayflies, Olives and a variety of Ecdyonurids. Trout are plentiful and fish can generally be found moving somewhere in the water. They are mostly free-rising trout too and dry-fly is usually a rewarding method of fishing for them.

On May 7th and 9th I caught many trout on the Hawthorn-fly and also had a few on it on the 8th. The smaller fish, I found, would take a nymph freely on those days but I wasn't going to put myself to the trouble of using a nymph as long as the Hawthorn proved so effective. Not until Tuesday, 10th May was I obliged to resort to the nymph for my sport, but when I did use it I discovered that it was quite effective, as the following extracts copied direct from my diary show:

Tuesday 10 May (1960)

An intensely hot day—the most oppressive yet. . . .

I went out after lunch and walked down towards the bottom boundary of the fishing. I was hoping for another good Hawthorn day but in the event it turned out to be like Sunday—very dead indeed. There was hardly a rise to be seen anywhere. The breeze, such as it was, did not seem to reach the water.

In these circumstances I decided to experiment with a nymph dropped into the quick glides at the tail of likely pools. The first throw produced a hard-fighting 9-inch trout and when I reached the next suitable spot where the water was funnelled from a broad pool under an over-hanging tree root, I got into a large trout for these waters —12 inches at a guess. I had this fish under control when, for some unaccountable reason, it let go.

I caught two more and returned a number of 6-inch fish, but very soon even the nymph ceased to move the trout. For the last two hours I was out, they were simply not interested. In the oppressive sultry heat I could hardly blame them.

Wednesday 11 May (1960)

After quite a wet night, we awoke to a damp grey morning. By the time I was up it had just about stopped raining, though the threat of more persisted all the morning. . . .

After lunch I went down to the seat by the river to begin fishing. I hoped to find the nice fish we've so often seen moving there during our evenings here. After several unproductive casts, I eventually took off my dry-fly and tied on a nymph because it seemed to me that it was too windy for spinners and I'd seen several rises at nymphs about to hatch, whereas the newly hatched duns, scattered by the gusty wind, hardly made it worth the trout's while to take.

This was the key to a wonderful two hours' fishing for, first chuck, I was taken by our old friend who went 11 inches: a good fish for the water above the bridge. I discovered I hadn't the washable lining of my bag with me so I had to come back. By the time I finally left the bottom pool I had two brace in the bag, and from then on, knowing I was likely to have a respectable catch, I returned everything below 8 inches, though I caught comparatively few small fish because by now I had a much better idea of the lies of worthwhile trout. By concentrating on these I picked up a dozen decent trout altogether, some of which fought with lively ferocity.

A word on the technique of nymph fishing on this river. The short seven-foot rod is essential owing to the trees, etc., and as some casts are necessarily short, a six-foot nylon cast is adequate, indeed necessary. Only two strands equivalent to 2x and 4x, each a yard long, go to make this up. The thicker of the two must be thickly greased to provide a sighter. The thinner is well mudded to sink. This latter need only be done at the start, or if grease gets on to it, but the thicker strand must be re-greased quite frequently in broken water.

One has to expect the nymph to be taken almost as soon as it hits the water. Indeed, on several occasions my nymph was taken by jumping trout before it touched the water, so quick are they off the mark.

(I have never seen natural nymphs in mid-air, and doubt if the Torridge trout have either. As to why they took my artificial before it reached the water, your guess is as good as mine.)

Only in the slowest deepest water was animation necessary. It is nearly always possible to guess the lie of a good fish.

We caught a live male spinner this evening, two-tailed, very much larger than a Red Spinner but not quite as big as a Mayfly, with two dark spots at the top of the wings (*Ecdyonurus insignis*).

Thursday 12 May (*1960*)

It rained most of last night and this morning was very grey, damp and unpromising. By the time we'd had breakfast, however, the rain had stopped. . . .

After lunch I went up above where I had fished yester-
day. I collected a brace before Jimmy Douglas joined me
for a bit. I got another, lost two on a nymph I subsequently found to be barbless, then did no good at all for
a long time. I eventually discovered that two men with
machinery had been working up the bank ahead of me,
apparently grubbing up bushes.

I have no doubt that without fishing below the surface I
should have done very little during these last three days of
my stay, for I was fishing only during the afternoons while
my wife was resting. In the event, my artificial nymph
enabled me to enjoy some delightful and rewarding sport
with these hard-fighting Devon trout.

SOME AUGUST TACTICS

Nymph fishing can be a boon, indeed, to the summer
holiday fly-fisher. By August rivers in many parts of the
country are low and probably clear. On many streams,
especially those whose waters are not of a calcareous nature,
there may be little fly and so few trout moving as to make
fishing prospects appear hopeless. The situation may not be
as bad as it seems, not if the river does still hold trout,
provided that nymph fishing is permissible and you are
appropriately equipped.

At the end of July and the beginning of August 1961 I
spent another very interesting and agreeable week at Woodford Bridge. When I arrived I found the river low but oddly
clear, the colour of very dry sherry. The weather at first
was mainly bright but rather windy. Fortunately the breeze
was mostly blowing directly downstream, the way I like it
when I am fishing, either with the artificial nymph or the
dry-fly.

The trout all seemed rather jumpy and those lying out
in the thin water running over the shillets at once raced off
up-river as soon as I got within 15 yards of them, creating
bow waves as they did so and alarming others in positions
upstream of them. It took me a little time to get the measure

of them, so shy were they, and this was only possible in certain places.

I found that by judiciously approaching, taking care not to splash or stamp, and by cautious casting around vegetation screens, I could reach trout with a throw no farther than about ten yards. It is also true that in the prevailing windy conditions and the considerable overhang of trees and bushes, I left quite a few nymphs and a number of yard points behind to festoon the Torridge alders and ash trees. No matter, a good many trout appeared on the breakfast tables of the hotel during my short stay.

On this water an 8-inch trout is probably the choicest eating of all. Despite their comparatively pale-coloured flesh, Torridge trout are sweet and well-flavoured, and with a little salt and lemon juice, a brace makes a delicious breakfast.

Their fighting powers for their inches are quite remarkable and they spend a lot of time in mid-air when hooked. Like most wild fish they are quick in the take and you have to sharpen up your reactions if you want to hook a high proportion. A fish of ten inches is quite creditable on this water, though you may take several some days and better fish are caught above and below the bridge every year. When I was there in May 1960 I had an 11-inch fish in the hot weather just after Princess Margaret's wedding.

One hot bright August afternoon, towards the end of my short summer stay, the trout seemed mostly to be lying in thin water, testing my approach work severely. I brought in five brace for the table but had moved and failed to hook two others, much larger fish which I estimated to be appreciably better than ten inches. Each seemed to me to be a fish worth trying for again. They were both missed because they were lying in deep water in two pools some way apart, probably concealed under the shelter of old alder roots, and had half-risen to a nymph fished only about two feet down. This depth would have been adequate for most of the water I fished during my stay.

I did not forget them. I lay awake that night and

pondered how I should take them. I got up early next morning and took my little box of fly-dressing materials from the boot of my car, set up the vice in my room, and dressed myself a few size 1 nymphs, well wired to take them down quickly. When we returned from the sea later in the day I picked up my gear and made my way directly to the lie of the big trout farthest downstream. Now this was the place where I had missed a biggish trout in May 1960 (see page 146).

The weather had deteriorated and now, late afternoon, it was raining, windy and dismal; not ideal conditions for nymph fishing but typical, as often as not, of a fishing day in this country at any time during the trout season. Waves, no less, chased one another across the wide triangular-shaped pool. The river's main flow was down the deep run on the opposite side, taking then a right-angled turn towards me, approaching from my angle. My trout's lie was on the upstream side of the right-angle. There was a tangled mass of half-submerged roots and branches over the deep hole where it had its hiding place.

My first cast was whirled away by the wind. The nymph swung round on the end of the fine point in an unintentional shepherd's crook and pitched into the water several yards away from where I had intended it to go. There was a suggestion of a pluck at the dipping point almost as soon as it entered the water—surf might almost be a better description. I struck and hooked a trout, sizeable enough to keep but not the one I was after.

Before trying again I waited a bit until the wind dropped for a moment. Even on the wildest day the wind nearly always lets up momentarily now and again, so different to the unbelievably steady press you feel on your cheek when the Trade Winds blow beneath the Southern Cross. It is in these still rough but relatively less violent intervals that the nymph fisherman must take his chances.

When I cast the second time the nymph went out passably straight, just touched a bracken frond overhanging the water, then pitched in about six feet upstream of the root mass. In the slow current sliding round the pool the nymph had sunk to a depth of near four feet by the time the dipping point at the surface indicated that it had reached the crucial spot. Then I imparted the short, smooth, gentle lift which I reckoned would bring the trout out from its hide unless it was in a state of rest. At five o'clock on a wet August afternoon, I felt the odds were on my side.

They were, too. The trout came, and missed. The trout missed, not me. Swear as much as you like in nymph fishing. It is good for the soul, sometimes, but never, ever, lose your fundamental patience.

I gave the trout ten minutes both to reassure it and, I hoped, to key itself up for a sharper reaction next time. Despite the gloomy dripping day this period was not uninteresting for in those ten minutes I counted 23 different birds around or over the pool. Then I threw again, exactly as before. I saw once more the dull yellowish flash deep below the roots, struck quickly and felt the hook take hold. I landed the trout eventually by balancing it for a moment across the broad toe of my wader and flicking it up on to the shillets beside the pool. It was as long as my old water-bleached foot ruler, and in good condition.

I waded up the pool, crossed the stickle at its head and trudged through the stunted bracken across the rough mole-infested pastures to the tail of a long canal-like pool where lay the second monster seen the previous day. I grasped the branch of a young ash—you soon learn to find your way about these Devon river banks, and all the handy ins and outs—and swung down somewhat ponderously but quietly into the thin water below.

I knew the line of approach from the experience gained in previous sorties: across the stickle to the shillets on the far right bank; creep along these to the point where the water began to deepen; wade slowly ten yards up the pool beneath the overhanging turf; pause a moment to sight the alder roots under the steep far bank some way upstream, and gauge the strength of the wind in this rather more sheltered pool; and then cast, aiming to pitch the nymph so that it would arrive beneath these roots at a depth of about three to six inches.

For once the first chuck sufficed. There was no need to move the nymph. As it was approaching the critical location my dipping point showed the cast draw under a shade faster than the natural sinking rate of the nymph I was using. I struck at once, the little loose line was immediately taken up and my reel began to sing.

I went back to my hotel with the small trout and my brace of 12-inch fish, either of which would have done credit to a chalk-stream. It is remarkable what large trout there are concealed in waters of this kind. They may rarely show themselves but they have to eat, some time. When there is little surface fly, it is unreasonable to expect to catch them on the dry-fly, although in the Torridge, at any rate, some sport can usually be had by this method with more modest trout. In non-calcareous waters where such aquatic food creatures as crayfish, shrimp, snail and so forth are much less abundant than in alkaline streams, few trout, even these biggish ones, can afford to pass up opportunities like an artificial nymph presented close to their lies.

When the water is very low and clear, a cautious approach is essential, especially on a bright day. There are usually a number of rather small trout lying out in the thin water at the tails of the long pools. If unduly alarmed these rather furtive fish rush off upstream and in so doing may put larger trout on their guard.

I have enjoyed good sport in these conditions by wading cautiously up the deeper reaches of small rivers, taking advantage of the cover afforded by overhanging trees, both to conceal my own approach and to reduce the possibilities of trout seeing and being alarmed by the shadow of the cast.

In these circumstances it is sometimes possible to see the trout quite clearly and to cast the nymph in such a way as to interest the largest one in each pocket of water. Remember too that not all the trout may be lying out in an obvious feeding position. Always be on the look-out for the presence of cover likely to afford concealment for a large fish and cast your nymph in a questing way, searching the likely deeps and corners. Be on the alert for any sign, however trifling, of a take. It may be a slight acceleration at the dipping point, a sallow underwater flash, a suggestion of a swirl, or something which can only be described as slightly odd, but which, when you strike, proves to have been a taking trout. When a trout does take a nymph, there is nearly always something to betray the fact to you and in time you come to know and recognize the signs, if you watch for them carefully.

Trout lie under trees and bushes for cover. Odd food creatures come their way from time to time, falling from the overhanging vegetation, but for every insect, caterpillar and so on which you find inside them you generally find many others which are purely aquatic. Logically, therefore, the nymph fisherman stands an excellent chance of deceiving these feeding fish, especially as their tastes are usually decidedly catholic. They can rarely afford the luxury of being fussy about what they eat, as the autopsies on them tell you later.

Tackle designed for fishing chalk-streams or larger rivers may be unsuitable for nymph fishing in smaller streams much overhung by trees and bushes. I have had satisfactory sport in these conditions on a 7-foot rod with a shortish cast of about 7 feet 6 inches. This is a little long in relation to the rod but for nymph fishing I always like 3 feet of fine nylon on the point.

On a hot day it is cool beneath the shade of the trees. The river too is soothing. If the heat is intense and you fish without a coat, wear a shirt of appropriate tone. You may find fish moving quite early in the morning and have better sport then than during the heat of the afternoon. Even in August, however, it is rare not to find some fish moving during the course of the day.

Nymph Fishing in Lakes and Pits

WHEN IS THE NYMPH EFFECTIVE?

THE effectiveness of an artificial nymph of the kind I employ varies a good deal in still waters. This artificial is after all an imitation of the nymph of an upwinged fly. The imitation serves perfectly well when dressed on a hook of appropriate size to represent any of the thirteen different Baëtid species (14 if you want to be pedantic and think you can distinguish between *B. vernus* and *B. tenax*).

Such an artificial stands an excellent chance of deceiving trout accustomed to seeing the nymphs of this agile darter group. None of the true *Baëtis* species are found in still water. Indeed as I explained in Chapter One, the nymphs of these, Olives, Iron Blues and the Pale Watery are physiologically incapable of survival in such conditions. The more robust species of the Baëtid family, the Spurwings, Slow- and Deep-water Olives, are, of course, better adapted to life in still water. That remarkably ubiquitous fly the Small Spurwing, is found in some still waters and its extremely agile nymphs are no doubt familiar to trout and other fish living therein. Trout certainly stand to gain little in calorific advantage from pursuing these nymphs in open water. But Spurwing nymphs live among the weed, often in quite heavy concentrations as you may see for yourself if you carefully examine weed specimens and record the tally of invertebrates you find among them.

Trout chivvy Spurwing nymphs out of their weedy sanctuary at times and fish in this hunting mood are decidedly susceptible to deception by an artificial nymph. Moreover, in favourable conditions of light, background and clear water, it is sometimes possible to watch the whole process of presentation, deception and acceptance and to time the strike accordingly. In lakes holding really large trout, this is quite a fascinating sideline of nymph fishing.

Provided the water itself is clean and unpolluted, ponds and lakes can generally be counted on to harbour the nymphs of either Slow-water Olives or Deep-water Olives, often both. These nymphs can stand quite a high water temperature and the nymphs of the Slow-water Olive are amongst the most robust and easy to raise under aquarium conditions.

Perhaps the most rewarding way to observe still-water nymphs is to study them in shallow lakes with a rough chalky bottom. The nymphs show up well against this white background and by alternatively observing and disturbing, a clear picture of nymphal movement and stationary attitudes can be built up. In these circumstances, too, mature nymphs can be studied as they prepare for emergence and in the actual process of emerging as duns. Although the same thing can be studied at home under aquarium conditions, aquarium and laboratory behaviour is no substitute for field behaviour, interesting and instructive as it may be.

In deeper and less weedy waters where nymphs may not be abundant and feature insignificantly in the diet of fish, it stands to reason that artificial nymphs are likely to have less appeal to them than representations of the food on which they chiefly feed, be it small fish, snail, freshwater shrimps, corixidae or caddis. The construction of such lures and the technique for fishing them is outside the scope of this book, but anyone intending to fish such waters, especially the great reservoirs of the Midlands and West of England, would be well advised to employ the artificial "nymphs", "flies" and "bugs" which have proved their effectiveness in practice and which are usually listed and recommended by the fishery authorities themselves.

Do not misconstrue my advocacy of a specialised, artistic,

and delicate style of nymph fishing as implying any doubt
as to the efficacy of larger lures. This is far from being the
case. When I go to fish big reservoirs, for example, and find
as I usually do that a great sea is running, the finesse of my
Netheravon art goes by the board, and rightly so. I use the
trick of weighting a biggish hook with fuse wire and cam-
ouflaging it with a bit of darning wool. This, I find, serves me
in good stead for fishing in still waters in which natural
nymphs play only an insignificant part in the nourishment
of the trout they support.

Remember, if and when you decide to employ an artificial
nymph in still water, to use it in those places and at those
times when trout may reasonably be expected to be alive
to the presence of natural nymphs active in the vicinity.

The nymphs which are commonly to be found in still
waters are those of species which have a likely emergence
period taking in most months of the year. In 1961, for
example, I recorded the emergence of the Small Spurwing
in ten months of the year between January 15th and December 22nd and the Slow-water Olive in seven months between
April 16th and October 27th. It therefore seems fair to
assume that nymphs of one or other of the usual species
may be present in the water most of the year, certainly
throughout the months of the trout fishing season.

But they will not be everywhere in the water. Slow-water
Olive nymphs are not likely to be encountered in deep
water, certainly not in deep weedless water. Deep-water
Olives, for some reason as yet unestablished with certainty,
prefer to live among milfoils and other weed in fairly deep
water, avoiding the shallows around the edges of lakes, ponds
and tarns. Spurwing nymphs, well adapted for climbing,
may be found among weed not far beneath the surface in a
variety of localities: they are, indeed, one of the most
ubiquitous British species.

None of these nymphs belong to the stone-clinging group
and it would be illogical to expect to find them present in
numbers on the exposed shores of stony lakes or reservoirs.
In my experience, nymph fishing in still waters is most likely

to prove effective when they are of limited extent, at least
partially sheltered, contain some weed, even if this is confined to sun-warmed bays and shallow areas, and support a
population of natural nymphs.

In recent years I have fished a variety of such waters,
stocked ponds, old-established, self-stocking artificial lakes
fed, of course, by feeder streams in which fish can spawn,
flooded gravel pits through which flow the headwaters of a
Test tributary, and recently created artificial lakes in which,
by careful plankton farming, large trout can be reared in a
short time.

From time to time I have enjoyed fascinating and rewarding sport in all of these on the same artificial nymph which
serves me so effectively in rivers and streams where the water
is reasonably clear and trout feed naturally on Ephemeropteran nymphs. A few of my experiences with still-water
nymph fishing, in practice, are related in the following
sections.

RAINBOWS IN A SMALL LAKE

In July 1960 Brigadier John Hopwood invited me to lunch
with him at Westbury and afterwards to fish the small lake
in Leighton Park where the Regular Commissions Board is
located. The lake had been stocked some months earlier
with assorted rainbow trout which were reported to be doing
well. It was rather a hot afternoon and it was about 3 p.m.,
Summer Time, when we walked down to the lake, our wives
following a little later.

The elongated pear-shaped lake, in a hollow surrounded
for about two-thirds of its circumference by trees, was about
80 yards in length and 30 yards wide, with an average depth
of about three feet. There was a good deal of weed in the
water with rafts of thick scum, intermixed with much weed,
dotted about on the surface. The water itself, although
distinctly greenish, was reasonably clear. After watching
carefully for a moment I could see several large fish cruising
on separate but intersecting and roughly figure-of-eight
beats in the middle of the widest part of the lake. Among

them were two fish whose weight I estimated to be at least two pounds apiece. The fish I felt sure could see us on the bank but continued to cruise purposefully about 18 in. below the surface, sometimes accelerating or swinging slightly off course as if to intercept some aquatic food creature. Despite the Brigadier's assurance, doubtless well-founded, that they wouldn't mind me standing up, I knelt down and concealed myself as best I could from sheer force of habit. The speed at which these rainbows were moving, as well as these sudden unexpected changes in direction, added to the difficulty of gauging a cast calculated to present my artificial nymph with pin-point accuracy, correct for range, line and depth.

As there was no current to overcome, I chose a tiny oo hook, carrying very little wire and the remnants of a couple of herls by way of superficial dressing. I was fishing with my usual three feet point of fine nylon.

My first cast was taken smartly by a very large fish which snapped up the nymph when travelling at speed, and on feeling the hook, as I set it, made one sharp rush to weed which broke my point before it ever reached cover through sheer brute strength. Clearly, for these fish, my point was altogether too fine. Since they didn't seem to scare easily, I didn't put on another point, but tied another small nymph on to the next short link, cast to the second good fish and induced it to take frontally after several attempts to persuade it to turn aside a few feet had failed to succeed. I didn't find the trout too hard to manage, though it took a long time to subdue and I had to hold it very hard at times to keep it away from the great patches of floating weedy scum which looked rather like yellow pancakes on the surface.

This fish was almost too big for my landing net but I got it out safely after some anxious moments. I was asked to kill the fish and to do an autopsy on it later and report my findings. The trout weighed 2 lb. 2 oz. It was chock-full of snail and its flesh was pink and firm.

I caught two other rainbows which I carefully released without handling and then succeeded in tempting the other big one to take a second time. It leapt high out of the water when I hooked it and ran hard towards the weed from which I turned it. It swung away at speed, leapt again, then once more rushed for the weed and this time I just couldn't hold it. It drove beneath the weed quite irresistibly and I knew it must break me as the cast could not be expected to tow such a dead weight of vegetation. It did.

I saw no upwinged duns hatch from the water but some Slow-water Olive nymphs darted away when I peered over the edge and the trout, no doubt, were quite familiar with them. An artificial nymph is probably not the most effective lure to use in water like this: a "fly" or "nymph" intended as an imitation of the more important aquatic creatures on which the trout feed would almost certainly be a better all-round proposition. But in the clear bright conditions prevailing on the day of my visit, nymph fishing provided an interesting and artistic method of taking the trout and the whole process of presentation and deception could be observed in detail.

THE NYMPH AFLOAT

Sometimes in recent years I have fished the nymph in still water from a boat. One occasion was at the time of the Game Fair held at Castle Howard in 1960. I had travelled up from Wiltshire to York during the day to stay with Colonel John Bade at Strensall. That evening he drove me out to visit some friends, Mr. and Mrs. Dick Churton at Elleron, about 40 miles away. There was a biggish lake in the grounds of their very attractive property and after we had had a dram together they bade me try to catch a trout.

There wasn't much light left but when we reached the water we could see an occasional fish moving here and there. Colonel Bade and I climbed into the boat and he took the oars so that I could fish. We are old friends and he is always a most attentive and considerate host. Before the light failed completely I decided to try a cast or two with the nymph. I moved one or two fish to look at it but failed to induce any of them to take until I put on my artificial Sedge. The trout were clearly cruising at considerable speed and would not take unless the fly was directly in their path.

In the dusk, mallard, teal and a heron passed close overhead and there were many owls, both white and tawny, calling from surrounding woods. Of fly I saw very little except a few Sedges, though the water, very deep in places, held a good deal of weed and might, I fancy, have contained the nymphs of Deep-water Olives, for I picked one Chestnut Spinner, the adult female imago of this fly, off the water. For the record, the stomach contents of the trout I caught on the Sedge were almost exclusively caddis larvae.

Towards the end of September 1961 I was invited to fish a private lake in Wiltshire with Colonel Bill and Lady Joan Gore-Langton. I arranged to meet them at the entrance to the grounds at 5.45 p.m. and during the course of the afternoon I loosened up on the middle Wylye some miles away, taking two nice pound grayling on an Iron Blue just above the place where the old hatches used to be at Bapton. On my way to our rendezvous, I picked a great many mushrooms which were abundant at that time, and also some blackberries to take home with me.

We duly foregathered and made our way to the boathouse where we parked our cars, put our tackle together and climbed aboard the boat. Lady Joan gallantly took the oars, Colonel Bill directed operations and I was bidden to fish. They had enjoyed several successful evenings just previously on this lake, taking trout from one to two pounds on Blae and Green, Mallard and Claret, and other conventional wet-fly patterns. They had kindly invited me along on this particular evening to give my little nymph a trial and I was very interested to see how the trout would react to it on this most tranquil occasion.

By inclination I am not a still-water fisherman. For me, the sound and movement of running water, clean running water, is an integral part of the charm of fly-fishing, but whenever I do fish a lake or pond, I find it so interesting that I am sometimes tempted to do more of it, if only to learn more. Certainly there is a great future in still-water trouting,

16. The Moment of Emergence: a Mayfly Leaving its Nymphal Shuck.

17. Choulston Reach, Netheravon, Epiphany 1962.

to which more and more anglers must inevitably look for their sport in the years to come.

There was very little sign of fly at this time, but here and there an occasional fish was moving, the rises indicating that they were cruising at steady speed. My chances turned on the possibilities of the trout being familiar with agile darter nymphs and their ways. The lake was mainly shallow and the water felt warm to the touch. The most likely upwinged flies to emerge from such a habitat would be Slow-water Olives and Small Spurwings. I saw several spent spinners floating in the surface film. I skimmed them out into the palm of my hand. There was no mistaking them: the beautiful Apricot Spinners of the Slow-water Olive. I felt then that the Lord would deliver these trout into my hand, as once he delivered the king of Ai and all that was his to Joshua and the men of valour.

We made for a line of stakes off the far shore. The water was oily smooth. Two fish were moving between the row of stakes and the bank about 15 yards away. Skilful rowing sent the boat gliding steadily into this quiet channel and I cast to the nearest fish which moved to my nymph but did not take it. The second fish rose again within reasonable casting distance and I was able to drop my nymph in what I believed to be its direct path. The artificial had only just started to sink when I saw the cast draw smoothly down at the dipping point, struck, and was into a nice hard-fighting trout which just failed to register 1 lb. on the balance.

I put my scoop down the trout's throat after I'd killed it and discovered that the fish had been feeding mainly on Chironomid larvae not at all unlike my small brown artificial nymphs. I had no doubt that other fish feeding on these larvae would take my nymph readily enough provided that I put it to them sufficiently accurately. The rewards of such feeding are so trifling that fish cannot be expected to go far out of their way to obtain them.

Another fish moved in the space between the stakes and the shore. In the reflected evening light it was impossible to see into the water although it was quite clear, and looking over the side of the boat I estimated the depth to be not more than two feet. As I was getting out line to cast to the last rise, the trout moved again, evidently just beneath the surface, and I was able to put my nymph very close to it indeed. Again the cast drew under and this time I was into a better fish which proved to weigh 2 lb. 1 oz.

I stopped fishing after this and thereafter acted as spotter in my turn. It is always very interesting to employ the nymph in unfamiliar circumstances and I have the most agreeable memories of our fishing on that peaceful evening.

A MIXED BAG

In the last ten days of August 1961, I took good trout from a variety of rivers. They were my principal quarry then, but I also had a number of respectable grayling, the best from Abbot's Barton being half an ounce under two pounds. My heaviest fish, however, was a chub.

I had reserved Tuesday August 29th to take my wife and daughter to Andover to catch the 12.59 train to London: the child was being taken to stay with relatives and I was to meet my wife when she returned alone early in the evening. I had some other business in Andover, but I knew I should have most of the afternoon free so I took advantage of a kind and long-standing invitation from Mr. George Walford to fish his water near the town.

The headwaters of the Anton flow through a chain of lakes developed from old gravel pits. After these were flooded the area became a sanctuary for birds and wild life and produced a most interesting and closely preserved mixed fishery with water of considerable depth in places. I had several times visited the pits with field-glasses, for I am as interested in birds as I am in fish, but I had not fished there before.

I reached the water about 2 p.m. on what was the hottest day of the year, and reputed to be the hottest August day for eight years, with temperatures approaching 38 degrees Centigrade (100 degrees Fahrenheit).

There were one or two trout on view at first, but as the heat became intense they seemed to disappear into cover. I could see no sign of surface movement anywhere, but I hoped to be able to interest any fish I could locate visually with a well-sunk nymph, for there were a few nymphs to be seen here and there around the edges of the water, darting off as I disturbed them. The fish in the pits would undoubtedly be familiar with these nymphs.

I knew there were some quite large trout in this water, though it was not to be my good fortune to see any of them on this particular afternoon when the weather was the antithesis of what I like for fishing. One trout lying stationary close to the bottom in about four feet of water allowed me to sink my nymph to a position about a foot in front of it and at its own level. Then, when I lifted the nymph slightly with my rod tip I saw the fish glide forward quickly. I was watching the fish itself and not my dipping point, but at that depth I noticed no indication of the fish opening its mouth to take the artificial. Nevertheless the presumption of a take in view of the forward movement of the trout was obvious and when I struck I was not surprised to find the fish firmly hooked. I was able to twitch it free, however, and it returned to the bottom, still lying in view but with a somewhat sullen expression about it.

I dare say I imagine these looks on the faces of trout, but it is no bad thing to strive always to think on the same wavelength as the fish you are trying to deceive. Imagination is an essential factor in anticipation, as I have stressed before. And I don't imagine the fish that I bring home.

In a deepish hole through which a little current seemed to be flowing I could see several nice grayling. I caught and put back two of these, employing the same tactics as had deceived the trout earlier. I then became aware of the presence in the middle of the upper lake of a huge stationary shoal of coarse fish, roach mostly, among them many specimens of 2 lb. and more, at a guess.

Again and again I tried to persuade these fish to take my nymph, but they wouldn't even look at it, let alone take. I

was beginning to think of giving them best, for under the
burning sun I was feeling hot and dry and rather tired.
Then, among the modest two-pounders I saw a fish much
bigger than all the others and this one promised slightly
better because it was actually on the move.

In reflected light I had only a partially obscured view of
the fish as it cruised gently just beneath the surface about 20
yards out in a channel between two rushy promontories.
It was a longish throw and I had to keep my back cast high
as I was getting out line to clear the tall willow-herb and
other thick bank vegetation behind me. My tiny nymph
on a 00 hook dropped about two feet to the fish's left but
it altered course, and although I could not actually see the
take I saw the dipping point indication and the cast slide
forward. My nylon point was of 2.9 lb. breaking strain,
but somehow it held as the fish charged off round the corner
past the rushes and into the open lake.

It stopped running after a time and stayed out in the
middle behaving rather like a big dog straining on the lead.
It was some time before I got the fish ashore and confirmed
my impression that I had hooked a big chub. It was too
large for my capacious net which had effectively absorbed
several 4 lb. trout in the months preceding. I therefore
quickly unhooked the fish and pushed it back into the deeper
water before the heat could affect it. Soon after this Mr.
Walford arrived to see how I was faring and he confirmed
that there was a chub in this top lake, known to weigh 5 lb.
8 oz. a few weeks earlier.

Shortly after this he drew my attention to a trout of about
a pound weight lying out on top of some thick weed in the
lower lake and clearly visible from where we were standing.
I dropped the nymph lightly just in front of the fish which
shot forward to take it smartly. Despite the opportunity to
do so, this fish fought on the surface instead of going to weed.
A little later I hooked a second trout to make up the brace
which my host invited me to keep and by then it was time
to go. As I walked back to my car I noticed great charms
of goldfinches busy on the downy thistle-heads and I picked

a huge mushroom the size of a plate and two "buttons", each as big as my fist, which I later ate for supper. This might have been a real dog day. Conditions could scarcely have been less favourable. Once again the little nymph had enabled me to spend an enjoyable, interesting and rewarding afternoon on strange water in unfamiliar circumstances.

★ 15 ★

When Grayling Stop Rising

THE "GUY FAWKES' DAY" TRADITION

WHEN trout fishing comes to an end at Michaelmas
or soon afterwards, the dry-fly fisherman may
continue to enjoy some delightful sport with
grayling which at that time are approaching peak condition.
It is a mellow season and the sport is always linked in my
mind with the warm sweet smell of full barns and apples
in the riverside orchards, and of the curiously evocative
bittersweet aroma of harvest festivals. But soon there comes
a time when grayling show an increasing reluctance to feed
on the surface.

This is understandable. The heavy and prolonged
hatches of duns which are often characteristic of September
and early October fall off eventually, perhaps giving way
to a short early afternoon hatch which may not be of
sufficient intensity to wean more than an occasional fish
away from the prolific sub-surface feed available at this time
of the year. Dry-fly fishing ceases to be rewarding once this
happens and you must turn to the nymph or the sunk fly
if you wish to make a basket of grayling from a river where
fly only is the rule.

The point in time when the change-over occurs is variable
and rarely clearly defined. Guy Fawkes' Day is traditionally
the end of the dry-fly season in Wiltshire and, on the whole,
this has been borne out by my experience, but you sometimes
get days here in late November and, more rarely, in
December, when an unexpectedly heavy showing of duns
will once more bring the fish to the surface. Such a rise may

last half an hour or so during which some belated dry-fly fishing can be enjoyed. Such a day was December 16th 1961 and, indeed, I caught a brace on the dry-fly as late as' December 23rd that year.

On average you can probably hope to fish with the dry-fly rather later in the south than in the north. Even the rods who fish at Downton below Salisbury can usually count on later sport on the surface than those of us who operate above Amesbury.

You do not need surface movement to catch grayling at this time of the year provided that water conditions are suitable. These fish can still be caught on an artificial nymph for some weeks after Guy Fawkes' Day as long as the water is not unduly clouded as a result of wet weather or winter work on the bed of the stream. Moreover, grayling reach their best condition in late November, both as a table fish and as regards their fighting powers.

FINDING THE GRAYLING

At this late season the water has lost much of its clarity for the leaves have begun to fall and everywhere, both along the banks and in the water itself, there is an onset of decay. The ploughmen are busy too and heavy rains may colour the water slightly, making it difficult to see grayling when they are not rising to surface food. Living by the river as I do it is not difficult to keep track of the fish but finding them may prove to be quite a problem for the occasional visitor. Fortunately in late autumn grayling tend to congregate in a few favourite localities and these usually occur where a good flow of water runs into a pool sufficiently long and deep to hold the considerable numbers of fish which make up a shoal.

Some of these shoals may be very large indeed. On many occasions I have taken an average of 30-odd fish each Saturday from one favourite pool on the Upper Avon at Bulford, hardly moving more than half a dozen yards each time out. Men call this pool "Fool's Paradise".

Once the grayling have been located, it is important not to alarm the shoal. A cautious approach is always necessary to avoid scaring any outlying fish because if these rush forward into the pool, the whole shoal may take fright and mill around with every sign of distress. Any attempt to cast over them when they are thus disturbed may result in the furtive grayling quitting the run altogether. They should be given time to settle and resume feeding before fishing starts again.

With care, the shoal need not be disturbed at all. I am very particular about my background as I approach grayling, crossing and recrossing the river as necessary, and varying my position as the sun swings in the autumn sky. The words "always" and "never" are of decidedly limited application when speaking of fishing matters and hardly occur in this book at all, therefore heed me when I say never have the sun behind you.

Do not wear light or shiny clothing. Move as little as possible, especially if wading, and cast delicately. I use my normal ten-foot cast with at least a yard of fine nylon on the point. You can get remarkably close to grayling with care but you can only take fish after fish from the shoal if you ensure that they are not alarmed.

If the water is clear enough, it is interesting to study the individual fish in the shoal. Many will be lying quietly deep down among the shadows and some, the largest among them, may be difficult to see at all, hence the old name, umber, the shadow. Perhaps they are resting after feeding earlier while others may not yet have fed at all but will shortly start to do so. This is not speculation. You confirm these possibilities by examining the stomach contents of your fish when you get back home.

It is easy to discern those grayling which are on the watch for food. They constantly lift and turn in the water to inspect and perhaps to take some particle being borne over them by the current. Some of the better fish may be seen actively grubbing on the bottom for animal matter of various kinds. These large fish probably feed often for their stomachs are generally crammed with freshly eaten food. The stomach contents of a pound female grayling which I caught in the mill pool at Bulford on Christmas Eve 1959 consisted of: 159 freshwater shrimps, 13 snails of various species, two caddis, four Ephemeropteran nymphs, one dragon-fly larva, two large bullheads, a quantity of vegetable matter, and a half-inch long black pebble.

The study of the behaviour of grayling in a pool is also useful in planning the tactics for taking the fish with a nymph. Although the smaller, active fish may be seen taking naturals in mid-water and can be caught there or even just beneath the surface, the better fish will nearly all be well down and their capture depends on your ability to get your artificial down to them and your skill at making it behave like a natural nymph when you have done so.

THE NYMPH IN RELATION TO THE DRY-FLY

During the early part of November, grayling feed for much of the day, from about 10 o'clock in the morning to 4 in the afternoon, and their diet contains a high proportion of the larval forms of river flies, especially Ephemeropteran nymphs, together with many freshwater shrimps which are abundant at this time in alkaline waters.

We may deduce that nymph fishing is likely to be profitable up to about the beginning of December but that thereafter grayling are more likely to be interested in lures dressed to suggest other types of sub-aquatic food creatures, like those found in my Christmas Eve specimen: sunk flies, dressed for the purpose, or shrimp-like, quick-sinking lures. Your choice may, of course, be limited by the rules applicable to the water you fish. On the Upper Avon, for example, we are restricted to the nymph and our grayling season ends early on December 31st. Where the sunk fly is allowed, the rules may enable you to catch grayling up to mid-March.

Some idea of the relative importance of the nymph vis-à-vis the dry-fly to the regular chalk-stream grayling fisher may be gained from the following summary of my grayling catches for 1957–1961:

How taken	1957	1958	1959	1960	1961	Total	Average	%
Dry-fly	128	24	38	88	61	339	68	25
Nymph	560	151	222	98	145	1,176	235	75
	688	175	260	186	206	1,515	303	100

A few remarks may help to put these figures in perspective. Up to 1957, grayling were plentiful in the Upper Avon and that autumn I used to count on taking as many as 40 in an outing. But they were netted and electric fished so hard at the end of that season that they have not been anything like as abundant in subsequent years. Although I fish for trout in many rivers, most of my back-end grayling fishing is done in the Avon.

The apparent poor showing of the nymph in 1960 was due to the premature curtailment of the grayling season, in practice, by the onset of heavy floods late in October which resulted in the water becoming badly discoloured. In 1958, too, the water became thick and milky as a consequence of mechanical plant working in the watercourse higher up. When the water is discoloured, sport with grayling falls off completely on this river, and may not recover that autumn. It had no chance to do so, for example, in the great floods of 1960–61.

WEATHER CONDITIONS

Grayling are much more susceptible to water conditions than to variations in the weather. These they tolerate remarkably well. The relevant pages of my fishing diary for five successive but quite contrasting Saturdays in 1959 show this clearly. They may be summarised as follows:

Date	Weather conditions	Basket	Fly	Time caught
7 Nov	Fine, sunny, rather cold	30	Nymph, 30	1.30–4 p.m.
14 Nov	Dull, grey, cold, windy	15	Nymph, 15	10.15 a.m.– 1 p.m.
21 Nov	Fine, mild, bright periods	19	Nymph, 19	10 a.m.– 12.40 p.m.
28 Nov	Dark, windy, showery	11	{Nymph, 5 Olive, 6	12–2.40 p.m.
5 Dec	Cold, bright, frosty; all bank pools iced up	17	{Nymph, 8 Olive, 9	12–1.30 p.m.

This summary shows that it is possible to make a modest basket at this time of the year in all conditions of weather from mild to frosty and rainy to dry. Even so, a little sunshine helps as a rule. The times between which fish were caught show how they tend to feed later in the day as autumn progresses. I should make it clear that I began fishing fairly punctually at 10 a.m. on all five Saturdays.

Do not become impatient at this late season if you are not catching fish. This may take time as they may be slow to come on the feed, very slow indeed, some days. Until they do, you will catch few. Once they do, you may hope to catch plenty, if you are then in the right place and doing the right thing.

TACTICAL HINTS

Lunchtime break

The period during which grayling are willing to take may be short, so lose no time when it begins. If you start fishing at 10 o'clock and do not get a grayling until 12.45, you are asking for a light basket if you knock off for lunch at 1. If you aren't capable of delaying your lunchtime on a cold day, give up back-end grayling fishing altogether, or take the advice of my old friend Canon Robert Finch and carry a flask of hot soup in your bag. I carry a flask myself, though not with soup in it. If you are fishing for fun and fresh air, of course, it doesn't matter when you knock off, or for how long.

Outliers

There are times when quite a few grayling, especially the smaller, sweeter fish may choose to lie out on the shallows to feed in the gravelly runs between the starwort clumps and water-celery beds. They occasionally betray their presence by surface movement. Such fish are taking mainly Olive, Dark Olive, Small Olive and Small Spurwing nymphs. They are usually quick to spot a free-drifting artificial, accurately presented for line. If one cast fails to produce a voluntary take, try again, this time aiming for an induced take.

Deep pools

Most of the grayling, however, will be found in the long holding pools except for an occasional outlier which has dropped a few yards downstream, perhaps to search the ranunculus roots just below the lip of the pool. Now when fish lie deep, you must get your nymph down to them. A few fish may rise into mid-water to take but to do really well and set fish bordering on 2 lb. into a taking glide, you must present your nymph ahead of them at their level in the water.

You can't sink nymphs in a river like the Avon by sucking them or dipping them in glycerine. If this is the best the shops can offer you, stay at home or find some canal-like fishery elsewhere.

See that your nymphs are dressed over a core of fine wire or some equivalent which gives them the necessary sinking power. Even if you are not a fly-dresser, I strongly urge you to dress your own simple nymphs for grayling fishing. I used to tie mine long before I learned the elaborate art of fly-dressing.

When the nymph is being fished deep and slight lift is imparted with the rod to attract the large fish, the draw of the floating cast is usually followed by a slight pause, a very slight pause, before the cast dips sharply away from you with a pronounced tug clearly indicated at the dipping point.

During the split-second delay after the little draw you impart to the cast, the grayling is gliding swiftly towards the animated nymph down below, checking as it breaks hard with its fins to steady itself as it closes its somewhat turtle like mouth, with the overhanging upper jaw, over the artificial with a pronounced chopping snap. As it does so its own momentum, temporarily checked by the breaking action of the fins, enables it to follow through and planing forward, it pulls your cast after it causing the pronounced tug instantly recognizable by the experienced grayling fisher.

If you can get the timing right, you can judge the moment to strike automatically and can then proceed to take fish after fish from a deep pool without alarming the shoal in the slightest degree. When you have mastered this technique, keep yourself in practice by asking a friend who knows the form to accompany you. Fish blindfolded and then if you fail to hook a grayling after imparting take inducement, your friend can tell you where you went wrong—whether you were too slow or too quick in your strike.

Rough conditions

Who fishes for November grayling must expect to come up against the autumn gales. The take is easier to detect in wind-torn water if the cast above the fine point is thickly greased with mucilin, from a red tin. There are on the market today various other solid preparations made from silicones. I have tried only a few and they were indifferent, although I don't doubt have achieved astonishing things in laboratories. A cast thickly greased with mucilin, or whatever you believe works as a floatant for you, appears to lie in a little trough clearly defined on the broken surface of the pool, and even if the dipping point is invisible in bad light or driving rain, some indication of a take is nearly always apparent to a practised eye.

I find that grayling fight much harder in cold water than in mild conditions. Friends who have fished for them in the Austrian and Balkan rivers have confirmed this and the very experienced Scottish game fisherman, Mr. William B.

Currie, has reported favourably on the grayling fishing he enjoyed in Northern Finland.

On a crisp November afternoon after frost the previous night, the sporting performance of grayling is likely to surprise anyone who has caught them only during the trout season. The fish may play deep or leap clear of the water like a hooked trout. I have often known grayling leap three times in rapid succession on the Upper Avon in December. Yearlings which are pricked and missed celebrate their escape by skittering along the surface like the garfish you catch in the sea. Fish about 18 months old take time to tire and bring to the net although they only run three to the pound. Fish of about two pounds fight as hard as trout of that weight but may take longer to subdue.

Accessories

If grayling take freely, a capacious basket will be needed to hold them or, if preferred, a washable lining may be used in the fishing bag with, perhaps, an old-fashioned bass fish frail in reserve in the car boot. Grayling are wet and rather slimy to handle. When I am fishing for them I always carry a khaki cloth or dark green towel fastened at thigh level on my left-hand side. I use this to dry my hands after unhooking each fish because unless I am careful, damp and mucous may get on to the line as I draw it off the reel to make a fresh cast. Once this happens the line soon begins to sink and nymph fishing is altogether too delicate an art to be practised successfully with this handicap.

If fish rise behind you, turn and cast down and slightly across so that the nymph swings into them, wet-fly fashion. Grayling can rarely resist this stratagem and they take the artificial with a little splashy rise and a short pluck, both of which leave you in no doubt when to strike. What they take the artificial for I don't know. Not as a nymph, I fancy, nor is this nymph fishing for them.

Nymphing for grayling in late autumn is not only a rewarding sport from which many old people and others can hope to benefit by an occasional dish of delicate fish, but one which affords valuable practice and experience in this exacting technique. Grayling take a nymph quicker than trout and making a basket of them in the adverse weather conditions so often met with in November and December may teach you much which will help you to deceive trout in the untroubled sun-bright days of July.

It always surprises me that so few rods bother to fish for chalk-stream grayling. In my experience, good grayling fly-fishers—and they are few and far between—are usually good trout fishers. Except for one week in December when I was visiting my opposite numbers at the West German and Netherlands Schools of Infantry, I fished the Upper Avon for grayling every week of the grayling season of 1961 from October 6th to December 23rd. Fishing mid-week, when I could not be on the water, was Colonel Peter Hammond, the doyen of the Upper Avon. In all that time I myself encountered few other rods on the short length which we set aside for grayling fishing after September 30th. It is, however, significant that this small band of grayling fishers included several of the most successful trout anglers of the 1961 season: Mr. Michael O'Reilly, Dr. Richard Jones and Mrs. David Reid among them.

An appreciation

We have no monopoly of these beautiful fish on the chalk-streams. The record is held by Scotland: Mr. Stewart's magnificent 7 lb. 2 oz. specimen taken from the Melgum in 1949. The rivers of the Welsh Marches are renowned for their grayling: they know how to cook them in those parts, too, accompanied by a gentle mustard sauce.

My own favourite fish dish is grilled autumn grayling fillets and field mushrooms. The delicate flavour of the fish calls for an equally delicate but rather dry white wine. Chablis is a little too harsh. I make my own wine from the elderflowers in the Ablington copse parallel with Gunville hatch-pool, but only in those years when the second week of June is sunny throughout. There is a superb alternative, if you can get it, the somewhat flinty but very palatable dry wines from that part of Northern Bavaria which the Germans call Lower Franconia. These wines are so good that they are understandably loath to export them and you must go to Würzburg if you want to pick the best.

I have taken grayling as far west as the Tamar and they seem to be finding the Teifi to their liking in recent years. They abound in some North-country rivers and delightful accounts of the attractive grayling fishing in those parts regularly emanate from the pens of such grayling-loving tykes as Messrs. Tim Wilson, Eric Horsfall Turner and Arthur Oglesby.

The grayling's reputation is even higher in Europe than it is over here and Monsieur Charles Ritz gives it pride of place, pound for pound, among all the salmon family as a sporting fish. The fact is, I think, that few of us in these islands trouble to fish for grayling when they are at their best. When you have let off your children's, or grandchildren's fireworks on Guy Fawkes' night, pause awhile over your steaming punch, and think what else you might be missing between then and New Year's Eve.

EPILOGUE

As the grayling season draws to its close, the chalk-stream valleys take on a different appearance to that which lives in the minds of men who visit them only in the melodious flower-decked months of spring and high summer.

Apart from some scattered daisies and an occasional battered dandelion, few flowers bloom along the river banks at this time. Such colour as there is to be seen occurs mainly on the leafless trees and hedgerows: russet and cream tree fungi; rose hips, some still bright scarlet, others deepening to purple; dull crimson haws; and the curious pink berries of the spindle tree. From a distance, the willow spinneys along the Court Reach here have an orange bloom on them and at times, in bright sunlight, the bare beech woods are suffused with dark claret.

By mid-December trout begin to run up the secluded

shallow side-stream which comes in at Choulston. They spawn beneath the high bluff on the far side of the river. Each winter they make their way up to this quiet, shadowy place where the clear spring water flows along the edge of a gloomy fir copse beneath a steeply sloping bank to which cling old ivy-clad trees; ruinous alders and decaying willows, whose shattered branches straddle the stream. In the moist soil under the lip of this bank, hart's tongue fern grows, and moss, and dark liverwort encrusts the damp earth above the water's edge. Against this sombre background, the chalk-white gravel of the redds shows up in pale contrast, but it is here, amid the gloom and ruin and decay, that a new generation of trout will come into being in the weeks which follow Epiphany.

What, you may ask, has all this to do with nymph fishing? What do you seek when you feel a man's pulse? Surely not just to touch an artery but to feel the beat of life within. So it is with a sporting fishery. Many things go to establish and preserve it for your enjoyment. A river without birds and flowers would be a sterile place indeed. One might as well stock a swimming bath and write of fishing in that.

Dulcet, still, murmur the rivers of the Plain. Palliative their sound, like the soft, slow, soothing speech of the old shepherds, a few of which still survive on the sheltering, nurturing downs. Quiet, peace-loving men, with square, brown, gentle hands. Soon their ewes will lamb and they will know, as soldiers know, the diamond stars for ceiling, and take their time from the Great Plough orbiting in the wide northern sky, as courting foxes yap and yarr, and the white owl spreads her wings beneath the winter moon.

Postscript

WHAT, think you, passes through the mind of a man who writes such a book as this? Apart from his preoccupation with the routine affairs of his every-day life, is he cut off from reality, indifferent to the situation of others, living a pseudo-idyllic existence far from great cities, untroubled by the crowded pressures and conscience-searing questions of our time? Or is he, too, troubled in spirit, aware of the razor edge which separates peaceful co-existence from the holocaust of thermo-nuclear conflict? Does he not ask himself to ponder the sanctity of human life, however imperfect? And can he blithely ignore such issues as a man's right to earn his living to the best of his ability and give his family a full life, regardless of his creed and, more signi-ficantly, of the colour of his skin?

This is a book about nymph fishing and it is outside its compass for me to discuss let alone try to answer these questions here. It might be politic not to mention these things at all. It might be, but it would also be most un-realistic.

There is room by the waterside for every shade of opinion but I think there is no room there or anywhere else in the world today for brute indifference, except among men in whom there is no charity.

No serious work on game fishing can now ignore the gathering threat to the very existence of the sport as we still know it. Water abstraction, pollution, even rod pressure: these are only a few of the minor problems which neverthe-less affect us directly as fishermen and which we, as a brotherhood, seem reluctant to face up to. Some of the problems may indeed be incapable of solution but it is remarkable what can always be achieved by a combination of tolerance, co-operation and enthusiasm. We shall need to display all these if our fishing is to survive.

As individuals we can do little. Collectively we can do much. I therefore urge all anglers to join the Anglers' Co-operative Association and all game fishermen to support the Salmon and Trout Association.

I venture to hope that you have found something in these pages to interest or please you. Perhaps you are a man of affairs, bearing great responsibilities for matters on which you need neither my opinions nor my advice. Perhaps you are a man, or a woman, whose problems are much like ours. You must, I think, be a fisher or you would not have read thus far. And if, by the waterside, what I have had to say in the pages which have gone before helps you to refresh your mind and thereby enables you the better to take up whatever burdens await your return, then I am content. And may good fortune and peace attend you.

O. W. A. K.

Appendix

CLASSIFICATION OF NATURAL NYMPHS BY TYPES
(*British Species Only*)

Serial	Species	English name of dun	Remarks
	BOTTOM BURROWERS (EPHERMERIDS)		
1.	*Ephemera danica*	Mayfly	
2.	*Ephemera vulgata*	Mayfly	
3.	*Ephemera lineata*	Mayfly	Rare
	SILT CRAWLERS (CAENIDS)		
4.	*Brachycercus harrisella*	—	Rare
5.	*Caenis horaria*	Yellow Broadwing	
6.	*Caenis macrura*	River Broadwing	
7.	*Caenis moesta*	Black Broadwing	
8.	*Caenis robusta*	Dusky Broadwing	
9.	*Caenis rivulorum*	Brook Broadwing	A minute species
	MOSS CREEPERS (EPHEMERELLIDS)		
10.	*Ephemerella ignita*	Blue-winged Olive	
11.	*Ephemerella notata*	Yellow Evening dun	
	STONE CLINGERS—CLASS I (ECDYONURIDS)		
12.	*Arthroplea congener*	—	Nymph un-recorded
13.	*Ecdyonurus insignis*	—	
14.	*Ecdyonurus dispar*	August dun	
15.	*Ecdyonurus torrentis*	—	
16.	*Ecdyonurus venosus*	Late March Brown	
17.	*Ecdyonurus forcipula*	—	Only one record
18.	*Rhithrogena haarupi*	March Brown	
19.	*Rhithrogena semicolorata*	Olive Upright	
20.	*Heptagenia longicauda*	—	
21.	*Heptagenia lateralis*	Dusky Yellowstreak	Or Dark dun
22.	*Heptagenia fuscogrisea*	Brown May dun	
23.	*Heptagenia sulphurea*	Yellow May dun	

Serial	Species	English name of dun	Remarks

STONE CLINGERS—CLASS II (POTAMANTHID)

24. *Potamanthus luteus*   Large Brown-backed
                             Yellow dun   Local

LABOURED SWIMMERS (LEPTOPHLEBIIDS)

25. *Habrophlebia fusca*   —
26. *Leptophlebia vespertina*   Claret dun
27. *Leptophlebia marginata*   Sepia dun
28. *Paraleptophlebia sub-*
    marginata   Turkey Brown
29. *Paraleptophlebia tumida*   —   Rare
30. *Paraleptophlebia cincta*   Purple dun

AGILE DARTERS—CLASS I—LARGE SIPHLONURIDS

31. *Ameletus inopinatus*   Brown Mountain
                                dun
32. *Siphlonurus linneanus*   Large Summer dun
33. *Siphlonurus lacustris*   Large Summer dun
34. *Siphlonurus armatus*   Large Summer dun Rare

AGILE DARTERS—CLASS II—SMALL BAËTIDS

35. *Baëtis niger*   Iron Blue
36. *Baëtis pumilus*   Iron Blue
37. *Baëtis atrebatinus*   Dark Olive
38. *Baëtis rhodani*   Large Olive
39. *Baëtis buceratus*   —   Local
40. *Baëtis vernus*   Olive
41. *Baëtis tenax*   —   Like *B. vernus*
42. *Baëtis scambus*   Small Olive
43. *Baëtis bioculatus*   Pale Watery
44. *Centroptilum luteolum*   Small Spurwing
45. *Centroptilum pennulatum* Large Spurwing
46. *Cloëon dipterum*   Slow-water Olive   Or Pond Olive
47. *Cloëon simile*   Deep-water Olive   Or Lake Olive
48. *Procloëon pseudorufulum* Pale Evening dun

MAP OF THE UPPER AVON
(Officers' Fishing Association Water)

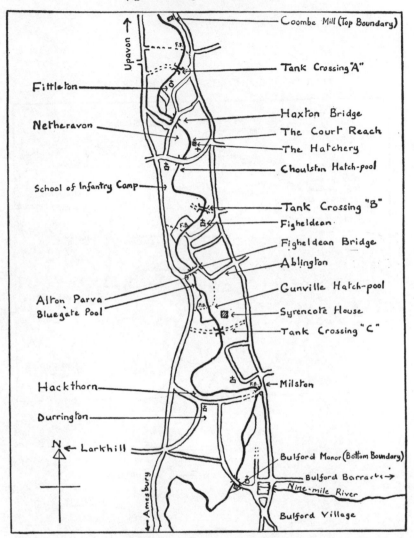

Coombe Mill (Top Boundary)

Tank Crossing "A"

Fittleton

Haxton Bridge

Netheravon

The Court Reach

The Hatchery

Choulston Hatch-pool

School of Infantry Camp

Tank Crossing "B"

Figheldean

Figheldean Bridge

Ablington

Gunville Hatch-pool

Alton Parva
Bluegate Pool

Syrencote House

Tank Crossing "C"

Hackthorn

Milston

Durrington

N ← Larkhill

Bulford Manor (Bottom Boundary)

Bulford Barracks →

Nine-mile River

Bulford Village

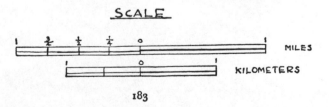

SCALE

MILES

KILOMETERS

183

MAP OF THE RIVERS OF SALISBURY PLAIN

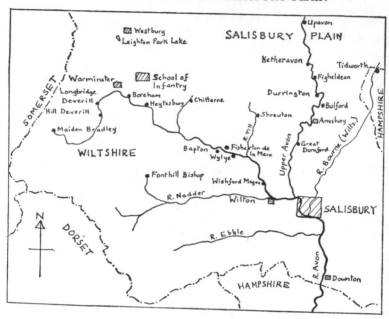

SCALE

5   0.   5
MILES

5   0   5
KILOMETERS

Bibliography

BERNER, L. (1950). The Mayflies of Florida. *Univ. Florida Studies, Biol. Sci. Ser.* No. 4.

EATON, A. E. (1883–88). A Revisional Monograph of Recent Ephemeridae or Mayflies. *Trans. Linn. Soc. (Zool.)*, Ser. 2. 3: 1–352.

FÄRNSTRÖM, N. (1960). *Öring.* Stockholm, Gebers. 1–157.

FOX, H. M., WINGFIELD, C. A., and SIMMONS, B. G. (1937). Oxygen Consumption of Ephemerid Nymphs from Flowing and from Still Waters in Relation to the Concentration of Oxygen in the Water. *J. Exper. Biol.* 14: 210–18.

GLEDHILL, T. (1960). The Ephemeroptera, Plecoptera and Trichoptera Caught by Emergence Traps in Two Streams during 1958. *Hydrobiologia,* 15, 179–88.

HARRIS, J. R. (1952). *An Angler's Entomology.* London, Collins, 1–101.

IVENS, T. C. (1952). *Still Water Fly-fishing.* London, Verschoyle.

KIMMINS, D. E. (1954). A Revised Key to the Adults of the British Species of Ephemeroptera, *Sci. Publ. Freshw. Biol. Assoc.*, No. 15: 1–68.

LESTAGE, J.-A. (1921), in ROUSSEAU, *Les Larves et Nymphes Aquatiques des Insectes d'Europe.* Brussels, Lebegue. 1, 162–273.

MACAN, T. T. (1960). The Effect of Temperature on *Rhithrogena semicolorata* (Ephem.). *Int. Rev. Hydrobiol.* 45, 197–210.

MACAN, T. T. (1960). The Occurrence of *Heptagenia lateralis* (Ephem.) in Streams in the English Lake District. *Wett. u. Leben,* 12, 231–4.

MACAN, T. T. (1961). A Key to the Nymphs of the British Species of Ephemeroptera, *Sci. Publ. Freshw. Biol. Assoc.*, No. 20: 1–63.

NEEDHAM, J. G., TRAVER, J. and HSU, Y. (1935). *The Biology of Mayflies.* New York, Comstock, 1–759.

PLESKOT, G. (1958). Die Periodizität einiger Ephemeropteren der Schwechat. *Wasser u. Abwasser.* 1958, 1–32.

PLUNKET GREENE, H. (1924). *Where the Bright Waters Meet.* London, Christophers.

RITZ, C. (1953). *Pris Sur Le Vif.* Paris, Librairie des Champs-Elysees.

SAWYER, F. E. (1952). *Keeper of the Stream.* London, A. & C. Black.

SAWYER, F. E. (1958). *Nymphs and the Trout.* London, Stanley Paul.

SCHOENEMUND, E. (1930). Eintagsfliegen oder Ephemeroptera, in DAHL; *Die Tierwelt Deutschlands und der angrenzenden Meeresteile,* Jena, G. Fischer. 19: 1–106.

SKUES, G. E. M. (1910). *Minor Tactics of the Chalk Stream.* London, A. & C. Black.

SKUES, G. E. M. (1921). *The Way of a Trout with a Fly.* London, A. & C. Black.

SKUES, G. E. M. (1939). *Nymph Fishing for Chalk Stream Trout.* London, A. & C. Black.

SKUES, G. E. M. (1951). *Itchen Memories.* London, Herbert Jenkins.

TILLYARD, R. J. (1933). The Trout-food Insects of Tasmania, Part I. *Pap. roy. Soc. Tasm.*

TILLYARD, R. J. (1935). The Trout-food Insects of Tasmania, Part II. *Pap. roy. Soc. Tasm.*

ULMER, G. (1929). Eintagsfliegen (Ephemeroptera) in BROHMER, EHRMANN and ULMER: *Die Tierwelt Mitteleuropas,* Leipzig, Band IV, Lief ib; 1–43.

WALKER, C. F. (1960). *Lake Flies and their Imitation.* London, Herbert Jenkins.

WHITNEY, R. J. (1939). Thermal Resistance of Mayfly Nymphs from Ponds and Streams. *J. Exper. Biol.* 16: 374–86.

WINGFIELD, C. A. (1939). Function of Gills of Mayfly Nymphs. *J. Exper. Biol.* 16: 374–85.

Index

Lane, Lt. Col. A. P., 128
Large Olive, 19, 36
Large Spurwing, 37
Larva, definition, 20
Larvula, definition, 19
Late March Brown, 33
Lateral drag, 70
Laverstoke Park, 105
Leckford, 68, 128
Leighton Park Lake, 157
Leptophlebia vespertina, 22, 35
Leptophlebia spp., 34
Limerick hooks, 43
Lines, 57–8
Longbridge Deverill, 139, 141
Lunn, A. W., 138

Maiden Bradley, 87
March Brown, 32
Marks, George, 102
Marrow scoop, substitute for, 63–4
Marsden, J. C., 105
Mating, duns with spinners, 23–4
Mayfly, 20, 26–8, 46, 54–5, 91–3, 127, 145
Measuring trout, 65
Melgum, R., 175
Meloy, Capt. Guy S., U.S. Army, 65
Metamorphosis, upwinged flies, 18–25
Microhabitat of nymphs, 101
Milbrolite rods, 59
Milfoils, 38, 156
Minnowing trout, attitude to nymphs, 75–6
Minnows, 75–6, 92, 94
Months when the nymph scores, 50–1
Moss creepers, 26, 30–1
Mucilin, 60, 139, 173
Mud for degreasing a cast, 61–2
Mushrooms, 131, 160, 165, 175

Nadder, R., 78
Netheravon style of nymph fishing, 55, 114, 124, 156
Nightingale, 96
Nine-mile River, 95–6
Normandy, 144
North Devon, fishing in, 144–53
Norway, 144
Nursery streams, 95
Nylon, cast specifications, 60–1, 147
  Knots, 60
  Menace to birds, 86
Nymph, artificial
  After Mayfly period, 93–4
  Animating, 77
  Anticipation in use of, 71, 114
  Basic requirements, 39–43
  Casting, 70
  Construction, 40–1

Cross-stream use, 69
Deep-water use, 80–1, 172–3
Detecting when fish take, 70–8, 173
Ejection by trout, 57, 70–1, 74, 77, 87, 129, 134, 141
Evening use, 78
Exact imitation futile, 21, 44–5
Hackle unnecessary, 41
Imparting movement to, 73–7
Pursuit by trout, 75
Prohibition of, 47
Reflected light in, 72–8, 136
Sawyer's method of dressing, 40
Sizes, 40, 54
Statistics relating to use, 46, 49–51, 67–9, 93–4, 170–1
Testing suitability, 39
When to use, 47–55
Where to buy, 46
Wire in dressing, 40
Nymph fishermen, trials of a, 115
Nymph fishing
  Accessories, 63–5
  Afloat, 159–62
  Approach work, 119–22, 168
  Bridge trout, 75, 85–6
  Bulging trout, 73–4
  Browsing trout, 124–6
  Carrier trout, 82–4, 125
  Choppy water in, 112–13, 139–43, 173
  Deception, 69–70, 74
  Deep water in, 80–1, 149–53, 172–3
  Detecting the take, 70–8
  Difficult places in, 82–9, 118, 122–3, 127
  Discoloured water in, 99, 170
  Dry-fly fishing, relation to, 45–54, 56–7, 68, 70–1, 169–70
  Ethics, 47–8, 54–5
  Flexible approach to, 49
  Gales in, 138–43
  Gravel pits in, 162–5
  Heat wave conditions in, 162–5
  Hooking fish, 70–2, 113–14
  Hot weather in, 105–10
  Influence of wind, 49
  Lakes in, 154–62
  Low, clear water in, 105–10, 130–7
  Non-calcareous waters in, 152
  Personal reservations about, 54–5
  Rainbow trout for, 157–9
  Rainy conditions in, 111–16, 139–43
  Reflected light in, 72–8, 136
  Rod tip control, 77, 87
  Snail eating trout for, 102–4
  Still waters in, 154–65
  Striking, 70–7, 113–14, 173